AF552681

PRINTED AT HOE & CO., THE 'PREMIER' PRESS
STRINGERS STREET, MADRAS-1

Appa began writing diaries as a college student, a ritual he followed till he was well into his seventy-fifth year. He would present family and friends with a diary each, published by Hoe & Co, every New Year's Day, writing a personal message, signing off with a flourish.

Eternal Romantic

My Father, Gemini Ganesan

Narayani Ganesh

Foreword by
Kamal Haasan

Lustre Press
Roli Books

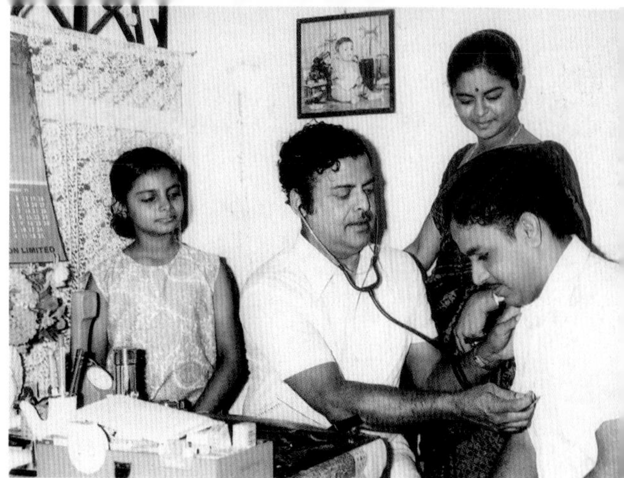

ISBN: 978-81-7436-578-1

Published in India by Roli Books
M-75, Greater Kailash-II Market
New Delhi-110 048, India.
Phone: ++91-11-40682000
Email: info@rolibooks.com, Website: www.rolibooks.com
Printed at Nutech Print Services, New Delhi

Contents

My parents at my workplace in Delhi, 1995.

Standing behind me from left to right are family friend Kamal Misra, Bobjima, TOI colleague Ratnottama Sengupta and Appa.

Acknowledgements

This book would not have happened if not for Khushwant Singh, who nagged me for over four years to 'just write it, my girl, it shouldn't take you more than a few weeks'. I am relieved that I no longer have to avoid the dreaded question, 'Have you done it?' that preceded greetings and pleasantries.

I have, as I often say, 'grown up with *The Times of India*', at my first 'real' job, where, for nearly a quarter of a century now I have learnt and unlearnt many things. Also, I have no hesitation in passing the buck to the TOI for leaving me with little time and energy to complete this earlier.

I am grateful to my family and friends who encouraged me to just 'do it' – despite my anxiety that it might fall far short of expectations.

'Kamal Sir', as Kamal Haasan is fondly addressed by colleagues, took valuable time off from his pressing engagements to say a few words spontaneously in a Foreword and I thank him for that.

Pramod Kapoor and Priya Kapoor of Roli Books have patiently waited, never once doubting that one day I would hand them a complete manuscript.

A special thanks to Swati Chopra for running her practised eye through the copy, nipping and tucking to produce a concise version.

Foreword

Gemini mama (uncle) was larger than life; there was so much more to him than his screen persona. That was what was so exciting – cinema was not his entire life, it was a vocation, a profession he chose over others. 'To me, life is oxygen, not cinema!' he would say. If he hadn't been an actor, he might have retired as an academic, with teaching stints in, who knows, Pudukkottai, Chennai, Delhi, U.K., U.S.A....

Could he have known he would become a popular hero, adulated and loved by perhaps millions, not just in India but in Malaysia, Sri Lanka and South Africa, too? He let his laurels rest lightly on his shoulders – to him, success was neither a crowning glory nor a heavy cross. And at a time when celebrities made it a point to publicise their acts of charity, he did it quietly, without fuss.

I touched and felt film 'stars' for the first time in my life when I was three and a half years old. The stars were Gemini Ganesan and Savithri, and I was to play their son in the film *Kalathur Kannamma* ('Kannamma of Kalathur'). Till then, I had no idea that actors were flesh and blood humans – I cannot forget the experience as they held me close in their arms, their 'child'. I began addressing them as 'Amma' and 'Appa' on and off the sets. Once filming was over, Savithri Amma said she would keep me and I clung to her. I'm told I had to be 'weaned' away from my screen parents. I was forced to call Gemini 'mama' or uncle. I was disappointed when they had their first child – wasn't I their child? Even today, Kamala amma (Gemini mama's daughter, Kamala Selvaraj) refers to me as her father's 'first son'.

I will always be grateful that it was Gemini mama who introduced me to cinema. 'Grateful, my foot,' he would say, making light of my gratitude. 'You should thank Srinivasa Iyengar and Charu Anna (my father and older brother).'

Some decades later, it was the same Gemini mama who exclaimed, 'You said to me once that you didn't know how to express your gratitude, and today you have put me in that spot, I don't know how to express my gratitude to you!' I was humbled. This was when I roped him in to play

FACING PAGE:

Kamal Haasan with Appa

From the Tamil film Parthal Pasi Theerum *(1962) in which Kamal Haasan played the role of Gemini Ganesan's son, after a similar role in his very first film,* Kalathur Kannamma *(1960).*

BOTTOM:

Sharing a joke

Appa and Kamal Haasan shared a comfortable chemistry.

my father-in-law in the film, *Avvai Shanmugi*, when he was seventy-six. It was a character so romantic that he gets besotted with his own son-in-law in drag. I think he enjoyed the role – it tickled him pink – that came unexpectedly to him!

You know, Gemini mama taught me a wonderful thing – to cup my hand like a conch shell and produce a whistling tone through that. It was really difficult to do at first, but with practice, I'm pretty good at it now. Also, I was fascinated with the way he would plonk himself on a chair after turning it around, leaning his chest against the backrest and letting his legs fall on either side. The first time I tried to do it my trousers tore! Now, when I want to be careful not to crease my trousers, I sometimes sit like that, and I say, 'I'm sitting like Gemini mama!'

It was Gemini mama who introduced me to the director K. Balachander when I was a teenager. When K.B. said, 'But he's so young,' mama said, 'Oh no, he's a man!' When I grew up, suddenly, I found that mama and I had become friends. We would joke together, spend evenings together. Sometimes, after an evening out, he would drive us back home and say good night and shut the door, forgetting that it was he who had picked me up! I would quietly walk back home. The next morning he would telephone me and ask, 'How did you reach home?'

In the 1970s, on one of her visits to Chennai, Rekha said to me that she would like to meet her father. I asked Gemini mama if I should arrange for them to meet somewhere. 'Why? Just bring her home!' he said. When we reached, we received a warm welcome and Rekha was taken on a guided tour of the house by the children; they were talking all at once and Gemini mama was seated in their midst. I observed everything like a lizard on the wall, and after a while slipped out quietly. That was an interesting experience.

Working with Gemini mama was not like working with a big star. He was warm and spontaneous. He had lots of love and respect for talent. I featured in his only home production, *Naan Avanillai* ('I am not he'), and also in *Idhaya Malar* ('Flower of my Heart'), his only attempt at direction. Mama was restless; he was more at home in front of the camera than behind it.

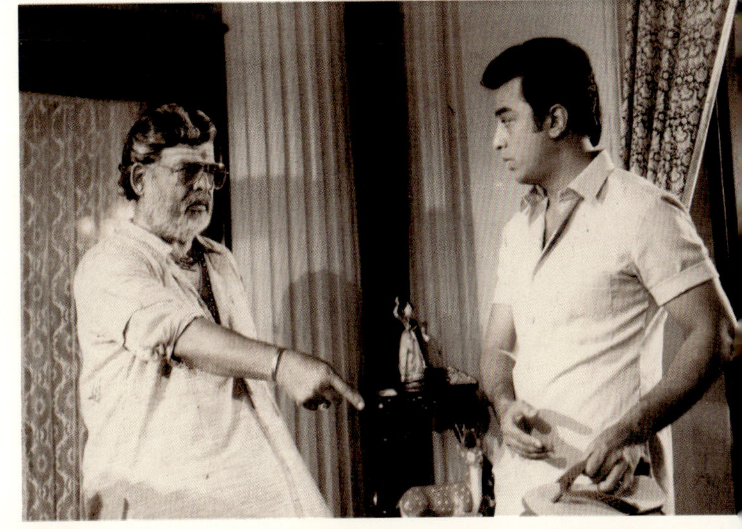

I was amazed to learn he was good at not one, but several sports – cricket, tennis, billiards, golf, even croquet. I once played a cricket match with him, along with M.A.K. 'Tiger' Pataudi and S. Venkataraghavan.

FACING PAGE TOP:
Rekha's first visit

Kamal Haasan brought Rekha to my parents' home in Chennai for the first time. Left to right: my sister Jayalakshmi (Gigi), my nephew Deepu, Rekha, Appa, Kamal Haasan and my niece Priya.

TOP AND RIGHT:
Rebellious son

Appa and Kamal Haasan in Unnal Mudiyum Thambi *(1988) in which as the rebellious idealist, Kamal finds it hard to follow in the footsteps of his orthodox musician father.*

Tug-of-war

Kamal Haasan with his screen parents, Savithri and Gemini Ganesan, in Kalathur Kannamma *(1960).*

Gemini mama was greatly attached to his mother and family and yet he managed to let every one of them live their lives like water drops on a lotus leaf, undisturbed and free of cloying expectations. He, too, was like that – and in the end, he 'evaporated' beautifully, leaving us inconsolable at the thought that he was gone. When I went to offer my condolences to the family the morning of his passing away on 22 March 2005, what moved me more than the tears was the fulfillment I perceived on the faces of his wife and children, and the way the members of his extended family had all come together, sharing memories and emotions.

Many of his co-stars were there, paying their last respects, and the media reported that among his screen lovers, 'Avvai Shanmugi' was there as well. That was a compliment, immortalizing me as part of his long list of onscreen lovers! He would have thumped me on the back and had a good laugh!

A tribute is no biography, as Narayani points out in her introduction, so it is but natural that she writes of what she knew of her father as a daughter who 'had a ringside view of his life'. So if you are looking for a complete lowdown of Gemini mama's personal and professional life, you will be

Last major role

Appa, Meena Durairaj and Kamal Haasan in Avvai Shanmugi *(1996) a film based on the Hollywood film,* Mrs Doubtfire.

disappointed. However, it offers new insights into his personality, peppered with interesting anecdotes and incidents that make for delightful reading.

The Triumvirate, as they were known, in Tamil cinema – M.G.R., Sivaji and Gemini – are now part of history. While M.G.R. and Sivaji competed with each other, Gemini mama was busy giving jubilee hits, a class of his own. One day, however, we'll all be gone – Dilip Kumar, Amitabh Bachchan, Kamal Haasan -- and it won't make a whiff of difference to cinema as there will always be others adding value to the world of make believe.

Gemini mama was a scholar among stars, sports enthusiast, voracious reader, a sensitive artiste, and a witty and affectionate human being. He did lead a tumultuous life, in parts. He's also had the benefit of a family that stood by him just as he cared for and loved them, no matter what. He was by no means perfect. Who is? He was no Rama. Gemini mama was more like Krishna, the eternal romantic – he was in love with life and everything in it. That's how I'll remember him.

Kamal Haasan
Chennai
August, 2010

Introduction

Playing with baby

That's me in 1954, around five months old, looking bewildered as Appa coaxes me to look into the camera. Clicked at the first house he bought in Chennai.

One of the earliest memories I have of my father is of him asking me to show him my teeth. I was growing permanent teeth and he would inspect them regularly. He'd returned from an outdoor shoot one day when he caught me trying to climb a tree in the garden. Getting out of the car, he picked me up and swung me around as I squealed. 'Say eeeeee,' he said, doing the same in a mirror reaction to reveal a row of perfectly aligned, sparkling white teeth. Horrified that my two front upper teeth were parting ways, leaving an A-shaped passage behind, he whisked me off to the dentist.

He and I, we sat there, in the comfortable air-conditioned waiting room of the Japanese dentist who practised on Chennai's arterial Mount Road. Appa was leafing through the pages of *Life* magazine while I watched the receptionist who was trying hard not to stare at Appa. Soon, it was my turn to be seen by the doctor. He examined my teeth, his mouth and nose covered by a transparent shield. I was to wear braces that would push the errant front teeth back together. As we filed out into the waiting area, the receptionist winked at me and whispered, 'What a handsome father!' I smiled shyly as we went out the door, tightening my grip on the hand that held mine protectively.

Whatever one might say of Gemini Ganesan, one couldn't possibly grudge him two things – his candy-box good looks, and his sense of responsibility and affection for his family and friends. My mother, I'm sure, had a bagful of complaints. But she too would always stop short of overt criticism. She could not bring herself to do so, she would say, because it seemed churlish considering the warm and irrepressible human being he was. And that's a huge compliment, coming from a normally cynical person who has, let's face it, had to share her husband's affections with not one but several beautiful, glamorous, successful and independent women, who weaved in and out of his life and ours. And two of them had children with him.

As his daughter, I had a ringside view of his kaleidoscopic personality and life. Gemini Ganesan was a man of many lives, each more interesting than the other. I would often wonder how he managed his juggling act. 'I don't,' he would confess, opening his eyes wide and shrugging his shoulders. 'Things just happen.' To every one of his children he has, whenever opportunity presented itself, offered the following words of encouragement, 'Success often comes to those who dare and act; it seldom goes to the timid.' At the same time, he would advise us to be 'ambitious, not avaricious'.

My mother, T.R. Alamelu – she never did give up her maiden name – who was fondly called 'Bobji', passed away barely seven months after her husband, he on 22 March 2005 at the age of eighty-four, and she, at eighty, on 27 November the same year.

Appa is no longer with us in body but his inimitable spirit lingers on, as fragrance from an era gone by. The following pages will offer glimpses of a life that began in a middle class family in Tamil Nadu's Pudukkottai and went on to capture the imagination and adoration of millions. By no means an exhaustive account of Gemini Ganesan's life and work, this book is more a daughter's tribute to a father who was larger than life and who was loved dearly by family and friends.

CHAPTER ONE
Early Days

If you carry your childhood with you, you never become older.

– Tom Stoppard

Whatever I know of Appa's early days is gleaned from conversations I've had with him, his mother Gangamma, and her younger sister who we called 'Chinamma'. Some were part of bedtime tales; others were Q&A sessions with a reluctant Appa in his eighties who just wanted to be left alone. 'Don't force me to talk,' he would say, irritated. 'I'm so bored. You keep asking me the same things.' Other details were got from a sketchy autobiography that Appa agreed to around the time he began to fall ill, where he spoke of his life and times to Jayashree Vishwanath, a freelance Tamil writer commissioned by my sister, Kamala, to do an 'as told to' account of his life. The outcome was published in Tamil, titled *Vazhkai Padagu* ('The Boat of Life'), for private circulation among family and friends. I later translated it into English for the benefit of his grandchildren, many of whom cannot read Tamil.

Ganapati Subramanian Sarma, or Ramasamy Ganesan, was born on 17 November 1920 to Gangamma, wife of Ramasamy, in the former princely state of Pudukkottai, which was by then a British province. How he metamorphosed into *Kadhal Mannan* ('King of Romance') Gemini Ganesan is a long story, several stories, in fact. We could peek into his multidimensional life through the prism of hindsight, for he is no longer here to add that inimitable flavour that was his forte as an irrepressible storyteller.

His mother had crossed thirty by the time Appa was born; her first-born having died in infancy. She would go on to lavish all her love and care on her second and only child, Ganesan, the apple of her eye.

Appa was careful not to over-dramatize the characters he portrayed on cinema – something unusual in Tamil filmdom that thrived on theatrical display. In real life, however, he was drama personified. This is how he described his entry into the world to Jayashree Vishwanath, 'A loud and natural orchestra provided a dramatic backdrop to my entry into the world.

FACING PAGE:

Appa as a child

He is standing in front of his granduncle, Narayanasamy. His mother, Gangamma, is on the right and aunt Krishnaveni (Chinamma) on the left. After Appa's father's death, Narayanasamy became his guardian.

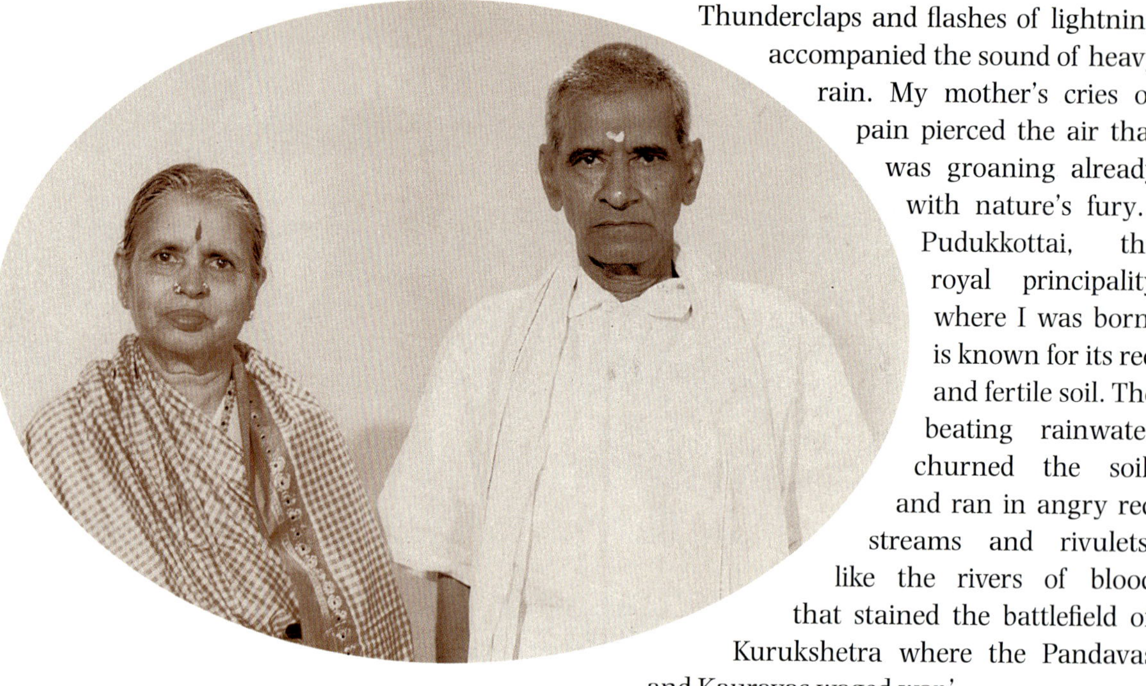

Thunderclaps and flashes of lightning accompanied the sound of heavy rain. My mother's cries of pain pierced the air that was groaning already with nature's fury... Pudukkottai, the royal principality where I was born, is known for its red and fertile soil. The beating rainwater churned the soil, and ran in angry red streams and rivulets, like the rivers of blood that stained the battlefield of Kurukshetra where the Pandavas and Kauravas waged war.'

Favourite Aunt

Chinamma and Chithappa, Appa's aunt and her husband, T. R. Ramachandran, who after retirement, came to live with us in Chennai. I was a baby then and Chinamma became my friend and confidante.

When Gangamma was in labour, her husband Ramasamy was so riddled with anxiety that his paternal uncle Narayanasamy – after who I was named – had to run around organizing everything. Like Krishna, the child was born at the stroke of the midnight hour, as the heavens opened up, sending the red soil of Pudukkottai helter-skelter in angry rivulets.

What did Appa's father do? Krishnammal, Gangamma's youngest sister, who came to live with us in Chennai after her husband, Ramachandran, retired, had a stock of interesting stories about the family. We called them 'Chithappa' and 'Chinamma', which was how Appa addressed them. 'Oh, Ramasamy would make music on his flute, wear silk *lungis*, *mulmul kurtas* and a thin gold chain round his neck. He was so handsome that when he walked down the street, women would ogle at him from their windows,' Chinamma would say. I would frown at her and insist, 'But what did he do for a living, Chinamma?' She would throw her head back and laugh. He didn't need to work, I gathered, as the family's needs were few and he lived off income from property and agricultural land.

Chinamma also told us that Appa was second-born. The first baby had died within a few days of birth. He was what they call a 'blue baby'. When Appa would trouble her as a child, she would tease him, 'Look at you, you look like a monkey. Your brother was so handsome, like a prince.' Chinamma herself wasn't bad looking; in fact I've caught her many-a-time stealing a look in the mirror as she went about her household chores.

Appa did the same – I once saw him drinking coffee from a steel tumbler, as all south Indians did and some still do, as he watched his own reflection in the mirror. He almost nodded in approval.

My mother, Bobji, was so unlike the Pudukkottai family. She was from Trichinopoly (now known as Tiruchirappalli), where her father, Rajagopalan, ran the railway canteen. He had extensive agricultural lands in fertile Thanjavur, some of which she later inherited. I don't ever remember Bobjima preening before the mirror – she was a shy, understated person, soft-spoken and submissive. In her later years, though, she displayed steely strength of character that saved the family from many a calamity.

Baby Ganesan was not only doted on by his parents, Chinamma and Chithappa (who had no children of their own), his paternal granduncle Narayanasamy too lavished affection on him. As an eight-year-old, the indulged child was to experience the tragedy of losing his dear father to a brief illness, and the bewildered mother-son duo, taken by surprise, were left clueless as to what lay in store for them in the future.

Extended Family

A rare photograph of Narayanasamy posing with his second wife, Chandramma, and family. Their daughter, Muthulaskhmi, India's first woman legislator and a pioneer doctor, is standing holding books. Son Ramaiah is seated on the floor.

Mother and son

Appa in a studio portrait with his mother. It was soon after he had recovered from a fever, hence the tired look, my grandmother would tell us apologetically. 'Otherwise he would smile a lot.'

Among the happy memories Appa had of his early childhood were his trips to the village tank with his friends. Appa would turn nostalgic, remembering how separate towels were earmarked for tank bathing as they would get 'dyed' saffron in the muddy waters. Filing home after a bath, the coloured towels round their waists, Appa would say they must have looked like a procession of young *sannyasis*!

Appa couldn't have known much about his father, Ramasamy, who passed away when Appa was barely eight years old. I would ask Gangamma, who we fondly called 'Amma' as he did, 'How did grandfather die?' All she could tell us was that he had very high fever and then he was no more. As a young Brahmin widow in conservative Pudukkottai, life couldn't have been easy for the thirty-something woman who was known to be the life and soul of any festive gathering. She was on the guest list of every family in town. With her long braid, exquisite jewelry and graceful demeanour, she was as pretty as a picture. She was a good listener, immensely popular among friends and relatives.

It was Chinna Thatha ('little grandfather') Narayanasamy who took charge of mother and son as a caring godfather, infusing confidence in the young child Ganesan, prevailing upon them to come and live with him at the 'Director's Bungalow' while he was principal of a college in Pudukkottai. He was also the founder of Maharaja's College, Pudukkottai, where a large portrait of him hangs, probably to this day. Ganesan was to draw great strength from this relationship, and till the end, made it a point to keep in touch with all the surviving relatives from Narayanasamy's second marriage to a non-Brahmin, Chandramma. He'd had two children from his first marriage, but both died young. Narayanasamy braved societal criticism with élan, standing by his choice, setting a brave example as a man of conviction.

A little digression here is necessary to complete the context of Appa's childhood. Narayanasamy had now not only become a father figure, he was also his mentor and guide. Narayanasamy and Chandramma's

TOP:

Childhood home

Appa's cradle at his ancestral home in Pudukkottai.

BOTTOM:

Gangamma's tulsi

The tulsi in the courtyard in Pudukkottai where Gangamma would offer her daily prayers.

Chinna Thatha's darling

Appa's granduncle (Chinna Thatha) who was Principal, Maharaja's College, Pudukkottai, seated in the centre with colleagues and students. In his left hand he holds a cane and his right hand is around Appa's shoulder. Appa is wearing his hair in the style typical of Brahmin boys of the period, with a tuft at the back and shaven portion in front.

Housing old memories

Appa's ancestral home in Pudukkottai

daughter, Muthulakshmi, became one of the first female medical doctors in India, founding the first cancer hospital at Adyar, Madras. She was also a celebrated social reformer and legislator, founding a girls' orphanage, Avvai Home, and fighting for the rights of *devadasis*. She married Sundara Reddy who taught anatomy at the Madras Medical College. They set up home in Madras where Appa would spend many weekends when he was a student at the Madras Christian College.

Narayanasamy's other daughter, Nallamuthu, went on to become the first Indian principal of Queen Mary's College, Madras. His only son, Ramaiah, however, died tragically at the age of thirty-nine, and Narayanasamy is reported to have lamented that the loss was too much to bear. So, little *pichchai* (alms), as Ganesan was called in Chinna Thatha's household since he was the only surviving male child in the family, took the place of the son he had lost, and became heir to some of Narayanasamy's properties. He was also given the task of performing his last rites when he passed away on 30 June 1930, when Appa was barely ten years old.

Gangamma would tell us that Appa was breastfed till the age of five. And she could only wean him after she began coating her nipples with neem oil. He was so attached to his mother that when he saw the barber sharpening his knife to shave Gangamma's head once she became a widow, he clung to her and refused to let the ritual take place. This went on for a year – he would wind his mother's long plait around his wrist at night when they went to sleep, lest she slipped away and got her head shaved. However, as was the custom among Brahmin widows at the time, she did the deed when he was away, probably at school, because she wanted to attend a relative's wedding and it would not have gone down well in the community if she had showed up with long hair.

Chinamma would say that Appa was a mischievous child, and would trouble her no end. He would insist she carry him on her hip, sideways, while she carried the pot on the other hip after filling it from the tank. Halfway home, he would undo her hair, letting it fall over her shoulders. Chinamma would have to plead with him to get down so that she could tie her hair up once more, as it was considered inauspicious for young, married women to leave their hair open. As a child, I would lap up these stories as Chinamma served us at mealtimes, or in the evenings once homework was done. And she had many tales to tell, including real-life ghost stories.

Chinamma and Chithappa came to live with us because Appa had insisted upon it, and he used their savings, to which he added some, to build a house for them near our home in Nungambakkam, Madras. This home was subsequently willed by Chinamma to me, her favourite grandchild. When they moved in with us, I was yet a toddler, and was cared for by Chinamma right through to adulthood.

I've heard about Appa's first day at school from Chinamma, chuckling as she relived that landmark day when her favourite nephew began his formal education. He was four years old. He was made to ride a horse to school, with a live band leading the way! Appa acquired instant popularity, of course, for his fellow-students simply loved all the fanfare and entertainment. The school was Kulapati Balaiah Primary School, at Nellu Mandi (paddy market) road in Pudukkottai, run by a Telugu-speaking Brahmin named Balaiah. Once Appa reached the school, Balaiah took him to a table on which was placed a gold coin and a silver plate. Holding the child's hand, he helped him 'write' Om in Tamil on the plate with the coin. Next, with *balpam*, a precursor of chalk, Appa was made to write the first letter of the Tamil alphabet on a new slate after Balaiah chanted a prayer and drew the Ganesa symbol on it.

Did the four-year-old cry on his first day at school? That is unlikely, with all the fuss and celebration. When I bought a perambulator (pram) for my first-born, Maya, Appa told me something I found really funny – that the gardener would wheel him in a pram to school daily! I guess it was not possible to ride a horse every day, and at that time, there were hardly any motorized vehicles and public transport, especially in those parts. But he did say that after a while, he was too embarrassed to continue with the pram as transport, and said so to his father who arranged to have him dropped to school in a bullock cart.

Appa's primary school

ABOVE LEFT:

The Kulapati Balaiah Primary School that Appa went to in Pudukkottai.

RIGHT:

Cultural influence

Town Hall, where his granduncle (his portrait is displayed on the wall here) would take Appa to music and dance performances.

Growing up in Pudukkottai, Appa would frequent Chinamma's place at Thirumalasamundaram, a neighbouring village, and also make trips to Dr Muthulakshmi Reddy's home in Madras. Appa had a cousin, Periasamy, who lived next door to him in Pudukkottai. They were close friends and shared a deep passion for cinema. The place where films were projected on the silver screen had three categories of seats – floor, bench and chair. Of course, floor seating was the cheapest and the boys were regulars every week, particularly to watch Hollywood action movies. Appa would say that during dramatic scenes, a live band positioned at the rear of the hall would begin playing, accentuating the suspense, fights, horror, or whatever it was that warranted more drama. The first film that Appa saw at Raja Theatre in Pudukkottai was probably Universal Pictures' *King of Jazz* starring Paul Whiteman with Bing Crosby making his first movie appearance. And the first Tamil film he saw was *Valli Thirumanam* ('Valli's Marriage'). He could sing from memory all the sixty-four songs of the movie. Once news of his talent spread, he was asked to perform for the Diwan of Pudukkottai, who was so pleased that he presented him with a silver cup.

When Appa was six years old, his father bought himself a bicycle for three hundred rupees which quickly became a talking point in Pudukkottai households. Appa would clap his hands whenever his father took out his cycle for a ride. Ramasamy had a close relationship with the tribals of the area, their common interest in quaint musical instruments brought them even closer, and he would spend hours listening to their stories and music. Chinamma would say that Ramasamy preferred the company of tribals to those in his own Brahmin community for he found them to be warmer and infinitely more interesting. Ramasamy played the mridangam, and he could never say 'no' to a tribal who came to sell him a mridangam. The result? His home had a roomful of mridangams of all sizes. He was also a keen participator in village sports like *rekla*, bullock-cart race, which is held in rural Tami Nadu usually during the Pongal season in January.

I remember Gangamma, Chinamma and Appa often recounting the prices of essential commodities from those years when salaries were in single digits and lifestyles were simple but wholesome. But, they would add, people were far more content than they are today, despite the conveniences, luxuries and sources of entertainment available now. In their early days, there was no electricity or piped water. Of course, no telephones, televisions or computers; no gadgets, no tech-conveniences.

Chinna Thatha got what was then considered a princely pension of hundred and sixty rupees when he retired. Appa's love for Shakespeare and

Like father, like son

Here he is, at home with the Kurava tribals who were keen to meet the actor who portrayed a Kurava character in the film, Kurathi Magan *('Son of a Kurava'), 1972. Appa's father would spend most of his time chatting and making music with tribals, and had a room full of percussion instruments he'd bought from them over time.*

Illustrious aunts

Left to right: Dr Muthulakshmi Reddy, Bobjima, Appa, Gangamma, and Nallamuthu Ramamoorthy (Muthulaskhmi's younger sister who was the first Indian principal of Queen Mary's College, the first government college for women in Madras.) Appa and Muthulakshmi were close and she was his mentor-guide in his growing years.

other literary figures, the importance he gave to education, and his flashes of non-conformism, were all due to the influence of Chinna Thatha. But it must have been his father's genes, too, that tweaked Appa's passion for outdoor sports, music, the arts, and his yen for daredevilry. Appa and Chinna Thatha would go to see dance recitals and listen to music concerts at the Town Hall in Pudukkottai. It was here that he first saw renowned Bharatanatyam exponent Balasaraswati perform.

Between school and home, little Ganesan had the opportunity to watch, and interact with, some interesting characters. Mr Iyer, a tennis champ, was popularly called *Kuzhandai* (Baby). His appearance was anything but baby-like. He sported a formidable moustache and in place of shorts, he wore a *dhoti* doubled at the knee while playing tennis. He even beat Capt. G.T.B. Harvey, the English tutor of Maharaja Rajagopala Thondaiman of Pudukkottai.

Appa's first trip to Madras was in June 1930 as a ten-year-old; he and Gangamma went along with Chinna Thatha to Dr Muthulakshmi Reddy's house to have him treated for diabetes. However, by the end of the month, he passed away, entrusting Appa in Muthulakshmi's care. So it was back to Pudukkottai, where Appa enrolled in the first form (sixth standard) in a school that was affiliated to Maharaja's College. No more horses and bullock carts, he now simply walked to school. Chinamma would recount that Appa would never enter the school through the main gate; he would jump over the wall. And so would get pinched as punishment by his teacher Venkatachariar, who would complain that 'the boy is very naughty and mischievous'.

His cricketing days began here, and as Appa put it, even before he went to college at M.C.C. (Madras Christian College), he was captain of the M.C.C. cricket team – Machuvadi Cricket Club, Machuvadi being the location! He began as wicketkeeper and went on to bowl and bat, and found that what he did best was batting. The school's Urdu tutor, Lateef, would also play cricket with the boys and would bring along a friend, Chinaswamy, who was a good singer. Between games, the boys would insist he sing for them. He was P.U. Chinappa, who went on to become Tamil filmdom's singing sensation. The early association with the talented singer brought a benefit – Chinappa gave the boys permission to stage his play, *Sangeetha Hridayam*, and the collection from it, three hundred rupees, went into the kitty of the fledgling, funds-starved Machuvadi Cricket Club.

During visits to Chinamma's home three miles away, Appa would watch as Chithappa assembled bicycles at the durbar office where he was a clerk. Appa treasured memories of how Chithappa would let him go for jaunts on his bicycle the whole day long, never mind the sweltering heat. At other times, Appa would go swimming in the two large tanks in the village. Later, in the heat of the Madras summer, Appa would wish a time machine could transport him back to those days so he could feel the tank's cool waters against his skin once more.

Muthulakshmi Reddy was by now concerned about Ganesan. Her father had entrusted her with the responsibility of the boy, but he was away in Pudukkottai. She began to insist that Gangamma and he move in with her. Sivakamasundari, Chinna Thatha's first wife, Gangamma and Appa had been living together in Pudukkottai since Chinna Thatha's death. Now, Gangamma and Appa set off for Vepery, Madras, and settled into two rooms in the annex of Muthulakshmi's home. Appa enrolled in second form (seventh grade) at Raja Muthaiah Chettiar High School, opposite Roxy Cinema on Purasawalkam High Road, which was not too far from home. They had one room to sleep in and another in which Gangamma cooked – because it was a meat-eating household, she would not eat from the same kitchen as her hosts.

Appa found his class teacher, Rangaramanujachariar, very interesting. It seems he was a Carnatic musician as well, and between classes, would often practise the veena in the staff room! On the other hand, Appa disliked the Sanskrit teacher, Krishnaswamy Iyengar, who was prejudiced against non-Brahmin students, of which there was only one in the class of twenty-two, Govindarajulu, who was actually excellent in Sanskrit. Appa would make a special effort to cheer up Govindarajulu. He would remember how his own father had felt more comfortable among the

Maharaja's College, Pudukkottai

The college was founded by Appa's granduncle and Appa went to a school affiliated to the college.

simple and talented tribals. And Chinna Thatha, who had braved social ostracism to marry a non-Brahmin woman.

We've heard a few interesting tales of life in the Muthulakshmi household. The first time Appa got a taste of meat was when Muthulakshmi's brother's wife popped a piece into Appa's mouth, saying it was raw banana curry. All hell broke loose when Gangamma came to know, and she lamented that an act of sacrilege had been committed.

Dr Sundara Reddy, Muthulaskhmi's husband, was a strict disciplinarian. He was dark-skinned and in college, students referred to him as 'Black Terror'. He was a devotee of the mystic Sri Ramakrishna Paramahamsa, and the children would tease Athai (Muthulakshmi), calling her Sarada Devi (Sri Ramakrishna's wife).

Not comfortable in Madras and missing her life in Pudukkottai, Gangamma said she wished to go back. Since Athai didn't want Ganesan's schooling to be interrupted once again, she admitted him to the residential Ramakrishna Mission Home in Mylapore. Here, Appa was initiated into yoga practice by a teacher, N. Subramania Iyer. He was also introduced to a formal study of the Vedas and the Bhagavad Gita. Though Appa found all this interesting, he missed his mother who he was very close to. He had never lived away from her for this long.

In a spartan room, with just a table and chair and a mat to sleep on, life was tough in the beginning for the coddled child. Appa would say it felt like he was on another planet. But he learnt some interesting things – his choice of vocational training was weaving cloth. In the evenings, he would learn yoga. Though yoga is best done on an empty stomach, the boys had to eat something at that time of the day, and so were given a light repast of wheat gruel.

Illustrious ancestor

Portrait of Appa's grand uncle S. Narayanasamy that hangs in the Town Hall, Pudukkottai.

All that he learnt and experienced at the Ramakrishna Home stood Appa in good stead in life, helping strengthen his body and mind to face the future. This is where he learned to be self-sufficient and independent. And he made some good friends who he kept in touch with for a long time. He didn't get much time to visit Athai, nor did his mother reply to the postcards he regularly mailed her. He was often homesick, and for a time learnt to live with it, but apparently not for too long.

Appa took lessons in Carnatic music at the Home and even won a prize for his rendition of

Vyasaraya Tirtha's composition, *Krishna nee begane, baro* ('Krishna, hurry, please come to me'), which he received from 'Tiger' Varadachari, a well-known exponent of Carnatic music at the time. At the Mission School, Appa participated in many plays. In one he was Lord Krishna, and had blue colour painted all over his body. His performance was much appreciated, and photographs were taken, he says, with magnesium sparks providing the light.

At the Home, Appa was privileged to hear Semmangudi Srinivasa Iyer sing live on stage. He had grown a beard at the time. Twenty-five years later, when he was a well-known actor, Appa happened to meet the singer again. He recalled the event and asked him about his beard. Semmangudi explained that it was during his wife's pregnancy; orthodox Brahmins grow a beard as a mark of celibacy during that period.

After completing the ninth standard, the homesick teenager finally decided to return to Pudukkottai to his mother and other relatives. Gangamma had taken a couple of tenants, and Ganesan was only too happy to be back. He'd said goodbye to the marble statue of Saraswati at the Ramakrishna Home, informing the goddess that it was his last day there.

It was back to the same school in Pudukkottai, this time in the fifth form (tenth standard). Then followed more cricket, cricket, and still more cricket, with Capt. D. B. Harvey as instructor. Matches were played between boys from the school and boys of the Pudukkottai royal family, the three brothers – Periya Dorai, Nadu Dorai and Chinna Dorai.

These cricket matches were interspersed with snack-time when they were served ice-cream, potato chips and cakes from the royal household. These occasions would sometimes turn into eating matches where the winner almost always was Ramachandra Shastrigal, a student, who could gobble thirty-two puris, twenty idlis and thirty helpings of ice-cream, all in quick succession.

Appa would often go along with the three royal Dorai brothers on hunting expeditions at night, much to the horror of Gangamma. She sat him down one day and explained to him that there was nothing heroic or sporting about killing vulnerable animals that came out at night to forage for food. And that was the end of his hunting exploits.

Once he completed his Intermediate (class twelve), Appa began to think of college and career prospects, and was given abundant advice ranging from medicine and the administrative services, to getting a basic college degree first. Next stop, then, was the Madras Christian College, where he enrolled in the B.Sc. Chemistry course.

CHAPTER TWO
College and Marriage

The whole of life, from the moment you are born to the moment you die, is a process of learning.

– J. Krishnamurti

The Madras Christian College used to be located at Parry's Corner, close to where the High Court stands today. First established in 1837 by British missionaries as a school, the institution was upgraded to a college in 1865, and renamed 'Madras Christian College'. A hundred years later, the College acquired four hundred acres of what was known as the Selaiyur forest estate in Tambaram. The institution shifted here in 1937, in a move that is still referred to as the 'great migration'. Here, Appa studied chemistry and after graduation, worked as a lecturer-demonstrator for some time before changing tracks.

Other reputed colleges in Madras then were Presidency College, Loyola College and Pachaiyappa's College, all exclusively for boys. M.C.C. was co-educational. Appa was a good student and sportsman and enjoyed the good things of life. The diary he maintained in 1942 has a few gems that reveal the kind of life he led as a college student. M.C.C. encouraged extracurricular activities for the all-round development of its students. Appa devoted generous amounts of time to sports like cricket, tennis, badminton and table-tennis; and also yoga, painting, playing cards, going to the movies, music concerts and eating out – all this in addition to being a fairly good student. In his diary, entries describing the above activities are interspersed with notes of his meetings with lawyers, relatives and others that reveal his family responsibilities; as also entries that record a bit of news from home about his mother, his wife, Bobji, and his friends in Pudukkottai.

Later, Appa became a regular in what we called the 'Hoe & Co ritual'. The company, Hoe & Co, produced diaries every year. After a page for personal memo, it reproduced Cardinal Newman's exposition on the 'True Gentleman', which included such gems as, 'The true gentleman carefully

FACING PAGE:

The newlywed couple

My parents soon after their wedding on June 30, 1940. Chinamma would brag that the ceremonies and festivities were held over five days.

TWO CENTURIES IN TRICHY MATCH

TRICHY, Dec. 8.

The South Indian Railway Ormsby Institute 256 for 2 wickets and declared (R. Ganesan 109 not out, including 11 fours, T. M. Dorai 102 not out, including 6 fours, C. Santhanam 28) drew with the Trichy United Cricket Club 80 for 5 wickets (Thambu Williams 25 not out, Andiappan 21 not out, Maharaj 2 for 27) in a match played on December 7 on the Puthur maidan.—F.O.C.

avoids whatever may cause a jar or a jolt in the minds of those with whom he is cast...his great concern being to make every one at their ease and at home.' And, 'He has his eyes on all his company; he is tender towards the bashful, gentle towards the distant, and merciful towards the absurd.' Also, 'He never speaks of himself except when compelled, never defends himself by a mere retort, he has no ears for slander of gossip, is scrupulous in imputing motives to those who interfere with him.'

The next 200 pages of the diary were devoted to the almanac, the *panchang*, postal and court information, listings of festivals, weights and measures, and members of government. It also had pages for milk and bread accounts. Then followed 365 pages, one each for every day of the year, and the last page was left to record 'Memoranda of things lent, etc'. The beginning of Appa's lifelong ritual was probably his M.C.C. diary of 1942-43, though he didn't begin keeping one regularly until 1946. No matter that some entries just said 'routine' or 'nothing in particular', and others were records of births and deaths, they contain interesting insights into his life and times.

Two newspaper cuttings from *The Hindu* – placed between the leaves of his M.C.C. diary – bear testimony to his cricketing career. 'Two centuries in Trichy match', reads the header, and the report informs that 'R. Ganesan scored 109 runs, not out, including 11 fours'. Another clipping titled 'Inter-collegiate Cricket' goes on to say that the M.C.C. team won 'thanks principally to an extremely plucky partnership between J. Basu, their captain, and Ganesan, who put on 66 runs for the sixth wicket, the Christians were able to save their face...at one stage they had lost half the side for 45, Ganesan hit out well and his 42 contained two sixes, the second one especially being a well-timed hook over the long-leg boundary.'

A Wednesday, 22 July 1942, diary entry reads, 'In the evening C. Rajagopalachari inaugurated the college union society, on 'how to speak'. People were disappointed because he never talked Pakistan.' Another entry reveals he spent two days painting. The entry, dated Thursday, 14 January, says, 'Busy painting. No other work.' And the next day, Friday, 'Busy painting. Completed the scene. Not bad from some distance.'

FACING PAGE:

MCC cricket team

Appa was captain of the cricket team at Madras Christian College, Chennai. He is in the centre, with teammates and coach. Below is a 1941 newspaper clipping from The Hindu, *reporting that R. Ganesan scored 109 runs (not out) in a cricket match.*

BOTTOM:

College colleagues

Seated on the extreme left is Appa with his colleagues at the Madras Christian College, 1942-43, where he graduated in Chemistry and also taught the subject for a brief period.

42 S. Padmanabhan,
8. Bazaar Road
Mambalam.

JULY 1942

Sunday In the morning went to Engineering College. Saw
5 Kumaraswamy. Had lunch with him. Then came
back to Adyar, went to Chellammal's house for lunch.
T.V.R's advice about my indifference! Then went to Guindy
Saw Venkatakrishnan. Had a walk to Adyar. Mangoes etc.
Saw S. Padmanabhan, then to Guindy. Had dinner

Monday Returned to Jambaram early morning. Class
began for Juniors. No real class. Receiving apparatus.
Morning V. Ganesa Iyer came to see me. Got a letter from
mother and also a mosquito curtain.

Tuesday
7 Last day for paying term fee in one sum or first instalment
No activities. Played tennis & cricket.
General body meeting

Wednesday
8 Played tennis.

Thursday
9 Played tennis. C.N. Subramanian, a student
of III BSc. wanted to have some chemistry tuition.

Friday
10 Tennis. Election meeting.
Lent Samuel Raj Rs 10/

Saturday Played a practice cricket match. Made 4 runs only.
11 Then in the evening went to Mambalam.
Saw K. Bhaskaran tried to ride the motorcycle.
Then saw V. Ganesha Iyer and Mani and came back

Sunday 12 Went to Madras. Saw 'Major Barbara' at Elphinstone. I felt awfully stuffy and sultry. Couldn't enjoy the picture. Then came back to Tambaram. Sent Jamdoss Re 1/.

Monday 13 Busy all day. Wrote a letter to auntie at Bangalore. Had some tennis. In the morning Dr. Ananthakrishnan came to my room 139. Advised me to take up some post graduate work and research.

Meeting of Senatus

Tuesday 14 In the morning went to the station with Kalyan to see Jayaram en route to Bombay. Class from 2-4. Had tennis. From last Saturday have begun taking eggs now and then.

Wednesday 15 Took oil bath. Got a cot in my room for Rs 2. Started to prepare quinoline in the laboratory. Class till 5. Then had some ping-pong & tennis.

Thursday 16 Continued preparation of quinoline. Had classes from 3-5. Boring. Couldn't play tennis due to rain.

Friday 17 → In the morning went to Bishop Heber Hall. Went to see Doctor about the 5 Rs he owes me. Went to college. Got a letter from auntie. Evening went to city. Saw 'Baktha [illegible]' free. [illegible] son was there as operator. That is why. Samuel Raj & I went to [illegible] afterwards. Had a nice time. Swell evening. Came back to Tambaram at 12 O'clock.

Saturday 18 Didn't go to the city. Played a cricket match. Only batted, did not do well. Played tennis & ping pong. Slight showers.

PREVIOUS PAGE:

College diary

Reproduced here are pages from Appa's MCC diary, recording his daily activities and thoughts.

College days were also when Appa saw a lot of films, and several entries mention the name of the movie with one-line reviews. Thursday, 21 January 1943, 'Went to city with Murthy... Saw *Pardon My Sarong* at New Globe. Abbot and Louis Castello. Nice picture. Went to Café Casino... Swell day.' The next day, 'Class work. Was talking with Catherine in the afternoon. Played some serious tennis and then some cricket. Framed a painting this morning.' And Saturday, 23 January 1943, 'Selaiyur Bhaskar Rao came to play old boys' match. We won; I didn't bat. Rukmini Arundale presides. Tamil farce was horrid. Nurjehan was not bad. Dinner. Gala day.' The Saturday, 6 March, entry records, 'Attempted some painting. Went to city in the evening to Roxy with Gurunandan Mulki. Saw *The Great Dictator*. Very good picture. Liked it awfully. Went to Hotel Brindavan, ate and came back.'

Between the 'swell' and 'gala' days punctuated by lots of sporting activity, painting, eating out and watching movies, a few entries refer to public speeches, strikes and rallies led by political leaders of that period, like C. Rajagopachari and M.K. Gandhi. For instance, Wednesday, 3 March, 'Gandhiji breaks his fast after 21 days. Nation's suspense at an end.'

Wherever the entry reads 'dull day', it also says it was raining. So, no sports! There are also faithful records of his weekly 'oil bath' and occasional trips to the tailor. It is obvious that college to Appa was not just bookish study. An earlier entry – presumably referring to his leaving his mother and other family members to board the train for Madras, on 24 June 1942, makes a mysterious reference to a certain 'P', 'Dep to go to Madras. Not v. happy. Took leave of everybody and boarded the train. P's last intimacy.' Did 'P' refer to Pudukkottai, or to a lady love? Who knows?

In a couple of days, however, back in the M.C.C. hostel, he is busy changing rooms, getting his tennis racquet re-stringed, visiting Rev. Boyd (the principal), going to the University Library, getting the scheme for the new academic year, and buying a railway pass for three rupees and eight annas. However, he also writes that he does not feel 'as happy as I did last year'.

Among my favourite recollections of the morning conversations Appa and I would have over tumblers of steaming filtered coffee – he in tennis shorts and I in a half-sari – seated on the balustrade of the first-floor verandah in our home in Nungambakkam, was the one we had about his roller-skating days. 'At M.C.C.,' he said, 'I would roller-skate in the corridors outside the classroom, between classes.' 'Really? Was that allowed?' I asked. 'Of course not,' he said. 'More than once I've just jumped off the first floor to avoid confrontation with the principal who was around the corner on his supervisory rounds. Other students would warn me that he was coming, but it would be too late to do anything other than jump.'

Naturally, I did not believe that he could jump off a first floor with roller-skates on. And old buildings have greater elevation than new ones. 'Oh Appa, how you exaggerate,' I exclaimed. 'How could you jump like that?' Before I could complete my sentence, Appa had hoisted himself on the balustrade, jumped on the sunshade and onto the ground below so swiftly that his reply, 'Like this!' came from somewhere between the first and ground floors! I was probably eighteen years old at the time and he, fifty. After that, I was careful not to provoke daring demos of this kind; it was much too risky.

Appa also informed me that even when he wasn't roller-skating, he rarely took the stairs; he would just jump off the balcony. When the Principal, Rev. Dr A.J. Boyd, learnt of these adventures, he confronted Appa and asked him if stories of his daredevilry were true. In reply, the young Ganesan demonstrated his skills by leaping off the balcony, much to Rev. Boyd's horror. He was marched off for counseling, with the Principal advising the student that if things continued this way, he would only jeopardize his own safety, for he might end up breaking a few bones. That put an end to his acrobatics.

The experience, no doubt, stood him in good stead when, on many an occasion as a film actor, he enacted stunt scenes without a double. Or so narrated his long-time driver, Sundaram, who was another source of interesting tales about Appa, especially from the film studios. Sundaram was hired when I was a toddler, and he continued to drive Appa and other family members for the next quarter of a century, first, in the Ford that was the family's first car, and later in other cars, including a Fiat and a Dodge.

One of Sundaram's favourite recollections of Appa's daredevilry was from a film based on a mythological story. In it, Appa was a prince who doesn't know his true identity. He scales a fortress wall, leaving his horse tethered to a tree below. On accomplishing his mission, he was to jump

Not just buildings

These are photographs of the MCC college buildings in the early 1940s from the personal collection of Tina Reid, a descendant of Professor Rev. J.R. Macphail, who was principal during the years 1956-62. 'These are not just buildings, they are a treasury of happy memories,' Appa would say.

Fitness routine

Appa was trained in yoga at the Ramakrishna Mission School where he studied briefly, in Chennai. He taught yoga at college, and continued to practise it well into his later years. These photographs were taken by Rev. J.R. Macphail at the Madras Christian College and sent to England for publication.

FACING PAGE:

Weighty matter

Appa doing weights on the terrace at our home in Nungambakkam, Chennai.

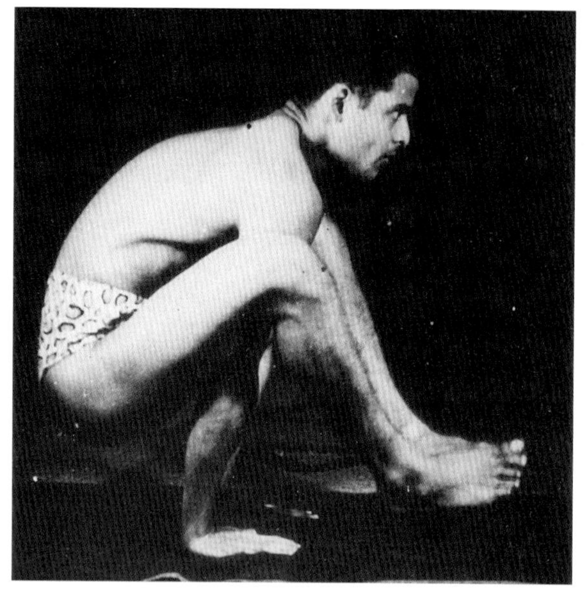

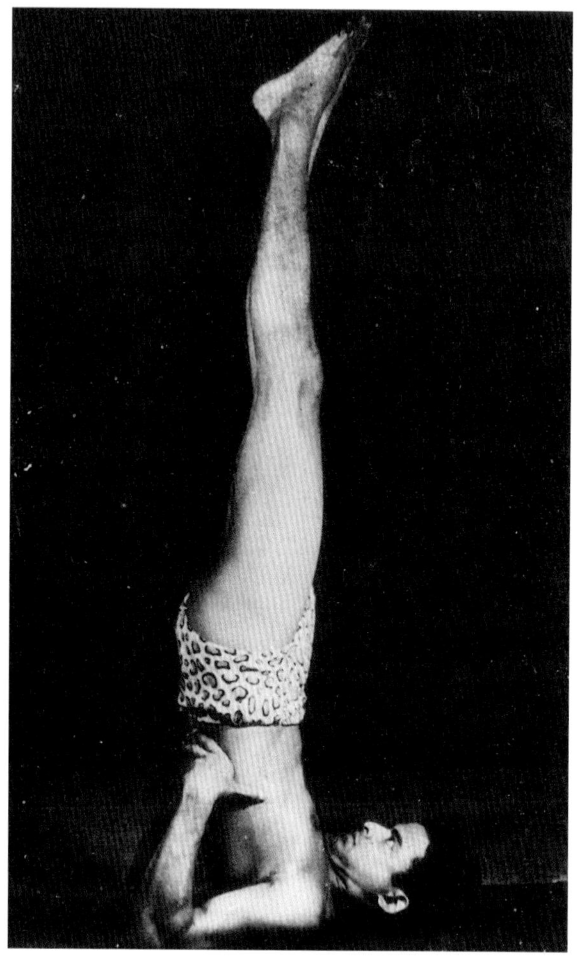

off the tall fortress wall on to the horse. Unfortunately, the horse broke loose and moved away, leaving Appa in a heap on the ground, considerably injured but with bones intact.

Chinamma once told me that Appa did not tell his friends and staff in college that he'd gotten married. One day, Bobjima's paternal uncle, Krishnamurthy – who I remember seeing as a child and who walked with a limp – was in Madras on a visit. He decided to look up his niece's husband in college. He was walking toward the college gate when Appa spotted him and ran to greet him. Appa cooked up an excuse for not taking him inside, and thanking the uncle for the sweets and tidbits he'd brought from Trichy, bade him goodbye right there, outside the college compound. It was probably hard for the handsome teenager to admit to his peer group that he was a married man!

Among the many close friends Appa made at college was a person whom he admired immensely for his creative enterprise and honesty. Jayaraman took care of the vegetarian section of the St Thomas Hall Hostel Mess where Appa had his meals. An incident in college brought them closer. 'I paid the mess bill every month,' Appa recounted. 'It was Deepavali time and Jayaraman presented me with a bill of sixteen rupees. In my accounts, however, the amount came to six rupees only. Angry, I flung the coffee I was drinking on his face and left in a huff. Back in my room, I was filled with remorse and regret. I sent for Jayaraman and when he came, I silently handed him five rupees. I didn't feel like confronting him. On Deepavali, Jayaraman came to show me the new clothes he'd bought for himself with the five rupees. I patted his back affectionately; we were friends once more.'

Later, Appa paid the entrance fee for Jayaraman to participate in a quiz organized by a Tamil weekly, *Ananda Viketan*. He won the grand prize of Rs 6,000, left his job and started his own hotel at T. Nagar, Madras, called Geetha Café. He never looked back after that. He opened a chain of small eating joints throughout Madras, all called Geetha Café. He later built Kanchi Hotel next to Ethiraj College in Egmore. Appa and Jayaraman would meet in their later years and recount their college days – Appa as a student and Jayaraman as a cook. They had an affectionate relationship, each admiring the other for his achievements.

While at M.C.C., Appa would regularly scour secondhand bookstores at Moore's Market – demolished since to make room for an extension of the Central Railway Station – picking up volumes on palmistry, chemistry, fiction, literature and poetry as well as biographies. When he felt homesick, he would visit Muthulakshmi Athai. She was an important influence in his life, guiding him when he needed advice and he looked up to her.

Railway canteen

Seated in the centre is Bobjima's father, Rajagopalan, who ran the railway canteen in Tiruchirapalli. Here, he and his colleagues are at a farewell before the government took over the canteen. On the floor next to him is his older daughter, Sethubai, who is five or six years old. Bobjima was born twelve years after Sethubai.

Appa was sports secretary and captained the M.C.C. cricket team for two years, winning matches also in table-tennis and tennis. He took up yoga seriously, and was so good at it that he was asked to model the various asanas. The photographs, taken by the 'last of the great Scotsmen at M.C.C.', Rev. J.R. Macphail, a professor who later became the Principal of M.C.C. from 1956 to 62, were even dispatched to London. Whether they were published or not, we don't know. At college functions, too, Appa would demonstrate yoga on stage; he also trained other students.

When he fell seriously ill before he passed away, the medical team that examined him said that his health had benefited greatly from long years of yoga practice and sports. Without that kind of disciplined training, they said, his body might have packed up much earlier. His hectic schedules as a busy film actor and later, the many emotional upheavals he suffered on account of broken relationships outside his marriage and immediate family, when he went through a depression that led to a period of alcohol dependence, could have taken a heavy toll on his overall health. But that did not happen and he lived to the ripe old age of eighty-four, loved and admired by family and friends, having provided well for all those near and dear to him in every sense of the term.

What was Graduate Ganesan's choice of career? He'd majored in Chemistry, and had worked for a bit as a Chemistry lecturer-demonstrator at the Madras Christian College, his alma mater. His father-in-law, Rajagopalan Iyer, who ran the railway canteen at Trichy, encouraged him to study medicine – he was willing to bear the expenses – but he died soon after the wedding. Bobji's only sibling, her sister Sethubhai's husband, died on 10 May 1941, and soon after, Sethubhai too passed away following a urinary infection, leaving behind a four year-old son, T.V. Ganesan. The boy was handed over to his father's brother along with whatever he'd inherited from his parents. Much as Bobjima wished to raise her nephew, Appa decided it was better to leave that to the uncle because he didn't want people to say he coveted the child's money and property.

Chithappa's brother, Narayanaswamy, was an officer in the Indian civil Services (I.C.S.). He advised Appa to either teach or join the civil services. Confused, Appa decided to join the Indian Air Force. He went to the interview in Agra despite apprehensions at home. He was the only potential earning member in the family and he had a wife and his mother to take care of.

At Agra railway station, Appa stood, bewildered, with a demand draft for three hundred rupees given to him to cover his travel expenses. He wasn't carrying any cash. Suddenly, a gentleman who had been observing the young lad came up to him and pressed some money into his hand for the ticket. He said he was going to Chennai, too, but after visiting Mathura and Bombay. Would he like to travel with him? Appa nodded, still confused. And so they traveled together to Mathura and Vrindavan, before reaching Bombay. At Bombay Appa stayed for a week with Baburao Patel, editor and publisher of India's first film trade magazine, *Film India*, at Matunga.

Appa narrated this unusual incident when I'd gone to Agra with him and my children, Maya and Sonali, in the late 1980s. Wasn't it dangerous for him to go off like that with a stranger? Well, Appa said, he was so kind and in my depressed state, he came like a cool breeze that soothed me, and somehow made me feel comforted, and I was confident once again, prepared to face whatever lay in store for me. Did he keep in touch with that kind stranger? No, he couldn't, much as he would have liked to, because he didn't have his address!

Though Appa was selected for the I.A.F., his mother was most distressed about her only child taking up such a risky career, and that laid the issue to rest.

Appa married Bobji on 30 June 1940, while he was still at college. He was nineteen, and she, fifteen. Bobjima would recollect, shyly, their first meeting. Asked to sing when the families met at her parents' home in Trichy, she sang a K.L. Saigal number that was a rage at that time, though she claimed she had no idea what the Hindi lyrics meant, '*Baalam, aan baso morey man mein*' ('My beloved, come fill my heart').

Bobji lived with her mother-in-law Gangamma, sister Sethubhai and three-year-old nephew Ganesan, in Trichy, in the house bequeathed to her by her father – while Sethubhai's husband worked in Salem and Appa was at college in Madras. In 1941-42, Bobjima was diagnosed with tuberculosis and was taken to the Perunthurai T.B. Sanatorium for treatment.

Cozy threesome

On the left is Bobjima as a little girl, seated with her best friend, Sharada, who is on the right. In the centre is Bobjima's older sister, Sethubhai, pregnant with her first and only child, T.V. Ganesan. The occasion is a baby shower, seemandam *in Tamil.*

A little digression here. Between Sethubai and Bobjima, seven children were born but none survived. So the age difference between the two sisters was twelve years. To ensure that this child (Bobjima) survived, according to prevailing custom she was 'sold' to their tenants and neighbours, Theekshappa Iyengar and Andal, for a handful of rice husk! And the child survived and was thought to be lucky, too, as her father's canteen business turned out to be a huge success, and he bought paddy fields of several acres at Mathrumangalam near Courtallam, and Eravancheri and Kadagam near Karaikal.

Appa's college diary records Bobji's progress at the sanatorium. He graduated in 1942, by which time Bobji had recovered from her illness and the family moved back to Trichy. This was when their first child, Revathi, was conceived, much to the displeasure of Sethu who was anxious about her frail sister's health. Appa joined the P.N. Raman Tutorial College in Trichy as tutor. Until Sethu died on 10 May 1943, they all lived at No. 1 Krishnan Koil Street, Trichy, in the house that once belonged to Bobji's father. Appa sold this house in 1970.

Revathi was born on 19 August 1943, and Kamala on 13 December 1944, at 16, Jaffarsa Street, Diamond Bazaar. Appa had to move to Dharmapuri because of a job as an assistant in the Central Excise Department. But in less than a year, he decided that this job was not his

Till death do us part

Bobjima and Appa on their wedding day, soon after the conclusion of the ceremony.

cup of tea. He decided to seek employment at S.S. Vasan's Gemini Studios in Madras because Vasan's wife, Pattammal, was a distant relative and she had mentioned that there was an opening that might suit him.

Thus began R. Ganesan's entry into the world of films, although behind the screen for the moment. He joined Gemini Studios as a casting assistant, responsible for selecting artistes who would work under the Gemini banner, much against Bobji's wishes. The family was in the process of moving to Dharmapuri, and she did not like the idea of her husband working in the film industry. Miffed, she went away to Trichy with her two daughters. Hadn't her father left her twenty-five acres of fertile land and a house? The plan didn't last. Frightened of getting alienated from her husband because of her opposition to his choice of career, young Bobji's resolve disappeared within a month. The entire family packed their bags for Madras – to an unfamiliar world and future.

Posing together

Bobjima and Appa in a picture taken by family friend and photographer, Rangachari, in Chennai in 1962.

CHAPTER THREE
The Big Screen

The only thing an actor owes his public is not to bore them.

– Marlon Brando

When did I become conscious of the fact that my father was a movie star? I do remember going to a preview show with the family when I was four or five years old, to watch a film that was to be released soon. The going was good until a scene where my father was being beaten ruthlessly by goons. 'Appa! Appa! Baaaaaaaaa...' I bawled, kicking and screaming, much to the embarrassment of my sisters and Chinamma, who were engrossed in the film. I was taken out of the hall and given toffees to eat, all the while being reassured by driver Sundaram and V. Mahalingam, Appa's manager, that it was a make-believe sequence; it wasn't real. I didn't stop crying till Appa was produced before me, hale and hearty, with no sign of a scuffle or beating.

I was born in 1953, and by then Appa was already playing lead roles in Tamil films. It was a meteoric rise for the young man who had joined Gemini Studios as casting superintendent in 1946. I managed to find records of how and when he landed the job, while going through a diary he wrote the same year.

On 19 June 1946, he wrote, 'Applied to the chief executive, Gemini Studios, and to the director of productions...' There is mention of an application to stage a 'social play'. Earlier entries record his various attempts to seek positions as Chemistry demonstrator at Vivekananda and Pachaiyappa colleges, between jottings about the movies he'd watched – *A Tale of Two Cities*, Louis Castello's *Naughty Nineties*, *Dr Kotnis ki Amar Kahani* ('The Immortal Story of Dr Kotnis'), and Corsican Brothers. He also mentions enjoying dance performances of Baby Kamala (who later became a renowned Bharatanatyam dancer, Kumari Kamala) as well as his appreciation of classical music recitals on the radio by veterans like T.R. Mahalingam, between shopping for saris and bangles for Bobji and voil clothes for the children, even as he tutored students at the 'Institute' in Trichy.

FACING PAGE:

Glamorous Gemini

A nattily dressed Appa in his early days of cinema.

On 19 July 1946, he writes about meeting S.S. Vasan at his home and there were discussions regarding the social play. Later, on 20 July, he records 'submitting to the ordeal of a make-up test'. On 25 July, Appa meets S.S. Vasan who appreciates his acting abilities, but tells him that the role requires an older person. Nevertheless, Vasan says he has the potential and that he should think about taking up acting as a career. 'Oh God! My thanks! Lead me straight!' says his last entry that day. He goes back to Trichy only to return to Madras after a couple of weeks, and formally joins Gemini Studios on 14 August 1946, as 'assistant in charge of the casting section'.

Appa's joining Gemini Studios is followed by days of shopping for clothes, hunting for a house, and meeting friends and relatives. He writes and receives letters regularly from Bobji, from his relatives in Trichy and Pudukkottai, and he records performing thread ceremonies and having oil baths on auspicious days as well as eating out at Udipi hotels, watching Hollywood movies, and witnessing the shooting of Vasan's mega production, *Chandralekha*.

Curly locks

Gemini Ganesan and his curls were inseparable, there were almost always a few spilling over his forehead. As children, when Appa would pick us up and hold us high in the air, we would gently pull at his forelock and watch as it sprang back on release.

Appa's first break as an actor came with the 1948 release, *Chakradhari*, starring Nagaiah and Pushpavalli who played the lead roles of a poor potter, Gara, and his wife, Thulasi, living in a village in Maharashtra. Gara is an ardent devotee of Lord Panduranga (Krishna). In one scene, he is kneading clay while singing the Lord's praise with his eyes closed, unaware that his little son is getting pulverized under his feet. The artiste who was to play Panduranga emerging from the clay was untraceable. Not wishing to hold up filming, Casting Superintendent Ganesan was asked to put on make-up and fill in. And that's how R. Ganesan came to act in movies for the first time, though it was *Miss Malini* (based on a story by R.K. Narayan), a social satire released first in 1947, again with Pushpavalli in the lead role, where he enacted a full-fledged role. The lead male actor was Kothamangalam Subbu, who played a villainous character who swindles Miss Malini of all her money. Appa's role was that of an assistant director of a drama

company, but the role got him acclaim and notice, and many film offers began to come his way. The titles listed him as R.G.!

With *Thai Ullam* ('A Mother's Heart'), released in 1952, Appa received critical acclaim as an actor, playing the villain convincingly. He had by then left Gemini Studios and was hired by the production company, Narayanan & Co., to act on a monthly salary. He was allowed to act in one film a year made by any other production house. On a visit to my home in Delhi, Appa saw a yellowing copy of Mrs Henry Wood's *East Lynne*. Excited, he informed me that the movie was based on this book. He wrote some words to that effect on the book's first page. In all, Appa acted in 180 films, in a career span of half a century. He did most of these films from the 1950s to the early 1970s, and his last film was released in 1998.

As an actor, Appa's USP was that he had a way with women; he oozed charm and with his candy-box good looks, wide-eyed innocence and gentle ways, he won over the hearts of more than a generation of

Handsome pair

Appa and Padmini as lead actors in Meenda Sorgam *('Paradise Regained'), 1960. They co-starred in several films that did well at the box-office. Padmini attended his grandson Rajesh's wedding in the U.S. in 1992. They kept in touch till the very end.*

fans. For them, he was the eternal romantic hero. They called him *Kadhal Mannan*, 'king of romance', a title he later claimed (when he was well into his eighty-third year) that he wasn't particularly 'proud of'. However, the fact remains that while his contemporaries, the swashbuckling do-gooder M.G. Ramachandran swung from forts and palaces rescuing damsels in distress and skipped around trees singing songs, when not uplifting the downtrodden, and Sivaji Ganesan delivered long and difficult dialogues and exhibited histrionics as *Nadigar Thilagam* ('the great actor'), Gemini Ganesan was wooing his heroines both on and off screen, kindling love and passion in the hearts of fans, young and old. And yes, considering that south Indian cinema then thrived on dramatic portrayals, his style was comparatively understated and subdued, since romance also often meant tragedy, either during the film or at the end.

This is by no means a faithful documentation of Gemini Ganesan as a film actor; neither do I claim to offer a critical appraisal of his films. This is the story of growing up with a star as a father, adored and respected by many, and perhaps disliked by a few. He might not have had the kind of fan-clubs that most organized stars (who had political affiliations) in the south had, but he did have a band of loyal followers who lapped up not just his films but also every detail of his life. Some became friends who kept in touch with him till he breathed his last, and continue to touch base with the family whenever there is an occasion to do so. Members of his fan-clubs had no formal political affiliations and neither did he, so they were free to bond as lovers of cinema and as individuals. In later years, they would often talk about their children, issues related to college admissions, search for jobs, for brides and grooms, the state of their health and who was doing what. It didn't occur to me then that his fan following must have been very different from that of his peers, most of whose fans doubled up as foot-soldiers in their political and public relations campaigns.

Shyam Sundar is one such loyal fan of Appa's. Recently, in 2010, his daughter got married and my sister Kamala was at the ceremony, 'on Appa's behalf', as she put it. When Appa's driver Nallasamy's son got married in 2008, I was there at the wedding in Chennai with my sisters, and was surprised to see a contingent of Appa's fans there, including Shyam Sundar. We were touched at the huge cutouts Nallasamy had placed strategically at the entrance, of Appa and Bobji, as though they were welcoming the guests.

There were two Ganesans in Tamil films at the time, V.C. Ganesan and R. Ganesan. V.C. later came to be known as Sivaji Ganesan (after his popular portrayal of the Maratha king), and R.G. as Gemini Ganesan on account of his early association with Gemini Studios. Fans of the other two members

RIGHT:

Krishna calling

Between shots at the studios dressed as Lord Krishna, Appa makes an urgent call.

BOTTOM:

Framed!

Flanked by Savithri on his right and Meena Kumari on his left during the filming of Missiamma. *The film was remade as* Miss Mary *in Hindi (1957), with Meena Kumari in the lead role.*

of the triumvirate, Sivaji and MGR, would sometimes yell out '*sambar*' at G.G. when he passed by, indicating he came from a Brahmin family fed on vegetarian fare! Appa didn't seem to mind, he found it pretty amusing.

Appa worked with some of the most beautiful women in his long career. Pushpavalli, Anjali Devi, Savithri, Padmini, Vyjayantimala, Devika, Saroja Devi and many others – too numerous to name individually here – were known not just for their good looks but also for their talent as actors and dancers. It is well known that he had more than a special relationship with two of them, first, Pushpavalli, and then Savithri.

Gemini in Durban

Visiting South Africa in 1973, Appa poses in front of the cinema hall named after him in Durban. It was built by R.K. Moodley, a South African of Tamil origin, a fan and dear friend of Appa's.

Appa's trajectory as a popular hero took off coincidentally in the year of my birth, and all through childhood and in my teens, what I saw was a handsome, much sought-after actor-father, always well turned out, exuding confidence and the fragrance of aftershave or perfume, with producers and directors lining up at our doorstep seeking an audience with him. His manager, V. Mahalingam, a law graduate, stayed with him throughout his working life. He was a stage actor too, and was affectionately called 'Mali'. Other members of his entourage were Balakrishnan or Baalu, an assistant, Parthasarathy or Paacha, another fan-cum-assistant, loyal chauffeur Sundaram, his make-up man of many years, Sundaramurthi. All of them would weave in and out of our house, checking call-sheets and schedules, booking tickets, organizing transport, fixing appointments. His life was one big whirl, considering he was also flitting between two homes and families, for by now he had another household with Savithri, and two children with her.

Each morning, Gangamma would lovingly extract the juice of pomegranate or sweet lime and give it to Appa in a blue-tinted Belgian glass. He would gulp it down, smile indulgently at his mother, and off he would go to work. If he spotted me around, he would ruffle my hair and tweak my nose, saying, 'Hey! What are you up to, eh?', and I would smile shyly at him, sometimes sticking out my tongue and waving my hand to say bye. Or he would pick me up and spin me around a couple of times and before I could regain my balance, he would be gone. Oh, how I loved him. So handsome, so charming, I would think, proud that he was my father. I, of course, was completely oblivious of whatever undercurrents there were at home, what with his extramarital relationship and flamboyant ways.

Brother Gemini

B Saroja Devi and Appa in the film, Kairasi, *1960. She adored Appa and respected him as an older brother. They've starred in several hits together, the most famous being* Kalyana Parisu. *She continues to be a close family friend.*

In the third standard at school, my Anglo-Indian class-teacher, feared by all of us in class, came up to me one day after school hours in the car park, where I sat waiting for Chinamma to pick me up. 'Listen child,' she said, 'your father has married actress Savithri?' I remember looking her up and down, and saying, 'Of course. My father marries all his heroines at the end of the film.' I was surprised she didn't know as much.

As a child, I have often locked myself in the large bathroom attached to my parents' bedroom to play-act in front of the huge mirror framed by bulbs. I would sit on the large blue barber's chair in front of the mirror, switch on the blazing lights, turn on the fan, and pretend to be Saroja Devi or Gina Lollobrigida, pouting and preening for minutes on end till my mother pounded on the door, wondering what was up. I would emerge sheepishly, after activating the flush, mumbling something about a bad stomach! I would sometimes leaf through girlie magazines like *Playboy* that I found hidden among the makeup trays in the drawers of that dressing table.

RIGHT:

Outdoor shoot

Photographed with the entire film crew at an outdoor location.

BOTTOM:

Fish, anyone?

Appa in a double role in the film Manam Pola Mangalyam, *1953, holding up a fish, striking a comic pose.*

Beauty and the beast

Anjali Devi in the lead role marrying Appa – who is disfigured due to a curse – in Kanavane Kan Kanda Deivam *(1955).*

For the next two decades Appa was among the top stars of Tamil filmdom. He had carved out a special place for himself as a romantic hero, and he won several awards for his performances. During this time he also acquired several properties, for he was not one who wasted resources. He wasn't cut out for business, but he knew he could invest in real estate as a safe option, and it turned out to be a wise decision.

Several of the films that Appa and Savithri did together were huge hits, like the 1955 release, *Missiamma* ('Teacher'), shot in Hindi with Meena Kumari as *Miss Mary* and in Telugu with Savithri and Nageswara Rao. The pair hit it off with the 1953 release, *Manam Pola Mangalyam*, loosely translated as 'marriage to a partner of your choice'. The film had Veena S. Balachander playing the role of the hero's friend, lending a bit of humour. The song '*Mapillai doi...*' ('Hey you groom') from the film became hugely popular.

Appa and Savithri acted together in forty-four films, and became popular as a romantic pair. She did many more films with other stars like Sivaji Ganesan, A. Nageswara Rao, N.T. Rama Rao, S.V. Ranga Rao and others. Appa was also cast with other leading ladies like Padmini, Vyjayantimala, K.R. Vijaya, Anjali Devi, Saroja Devi, Jayanthi and Sowcar Janaki. He did a few Hindi films including *Devta* (1956), *Miss Mary* (1957), *Raj Tilak* (1958), *Nazrana* (1961), and *Balaram Sri Krishna* (1968), working with Usha Kiron, Meena Kumari, Raj Kapoor, and Vyjayanti.

Why didn't he do more Hindi movies? Perhaps because he was a busy star by now in the Tamil film world and in those days, Hindi cinema was seen as just one more regional language film industry. Moreover, the Hindi films he did were remakes of Tamil ones. Appa was fluent in all four south Indian languages as well as in Hindi and English. He did a few films in Malayalam and Telugu. He took lessons in Urdu from a tutor as he got interested in the language, as a hobby.

Kamal Haasan made his debut as a six-year-old in the film *Kalathur Kannamma* – a 1960 release – that had Gemini and Savithri in lead roles. The film was remade in Hindi with Sunil Dutt and Meena Kumari as *Mein Chup Rahoongi* ('I Will Remain Silent'), in 1962. Kamal Haasan played the role of Gemini and Savithri's son who is brought up in an orphanage as the mother thinks her baby was still-born and the father is unaware that he had fathered a child. Savithri turns up as a teacher in the same orphanage and Gemini sees the little boy for the first time at a school play, since the school is run by a trust funded by his father. The family reunites after a great deal of melodrama.

Tragedy King

Appa, in a tragic lead role, with his 'son' Ramu in the film of the same name (1966). The morning shadow and kurta-pyjama were his trademarks while portraying the tragic hero.

As a youngster, Kamal Haasan acted in a supporting role in Appa's first and only production, *Naan Avanillai* – 'I am not he' – directed by K. Balachander and released in 1973, based on a Marathi play. In it Appa plays the part of a latter-day Don Juan, who woos and marries several women while he takes on as many different identities. He is taken to court in the end, but no one has been able to find out his true identity, as he speaks several languages with great facility. In the court building, someone slaps him (as it was felt he would utter something in his mother tongue when taken by surprise). But all are taken aback when he exclaims in a language that is not familiar to anyone. And so the mystery is left unsolved.

The film and Appa's acting earned critical acclaim, but *Naan Avanillai* did not do well at the box-office. He had named the production company, Shri Narayani Films. Throughout the years of my moving home from one city to another, the trunks that were used to store the film's spools came in handy to transport baggage. The lids of the trunks had the name of the company emblazoned on them, a reminder of his only home production.

I have heard Chinamma and Mahalingam lament about the money Appa lost in this film, but there was never a word from Appa. I think he immensely enjoyed the experience and he loved the story and his role as the protaganist, but wary as he was about risky business ventures, he never repeated the effort.

Naan Avanillai was remade with the same name by director Selva, with Jeevan playing the lead role with five heroines. Released in April 2007, the film has been described as a 'smashing hit' and now a sequel is in the making, continuing the story-line.

Kamal Haasan and Appa did a few movies together in later years, notable among them being *Unnal Mudiyum Thambi* ('You Can Do It, Brother') in 1988, and *Avvai Shanmugi* in 1996. While the former saw the two as father and son, the latter had them acting as father-in-law and son-in-law. *Avvai Shanmugi* was released in 1996 when Appa was seventy-six years old. In it, he falls for Avvai Shanmugi's charms, the nanny who is in fact his son-in-law in drag. The story borrowed heavily from the

In-laws on screen

Appa and Kamal Haasan in drag as Avvai Shanmugi in the film of that name, where Appa is the father-in-law and Kamal Haasan, his son-in-law.

Reel professor

Appa in the title role and Sharada, three-time National Award-winning actress, in the film Professor *(1972).*

Hollywood film, *Mrs Doubtfire*. It did well, what with the unusual theme and Kamal Haasan's performance. Appa's portrayal of a patriarch who finds it hard to resist the nanny's charms was widely appreciated. The film was subsequently remade in Hindi as *Chachi 420* with Amrish Puri playing Appa's role.

Appa did many films with the director K. Balachander, some of which stood out both in terms of story line and performances. In *Iru Kodugal* ('Two Lines') he is first a young I.A.S. aspirant who falls in love with Sowcar Janaki in Varanasi. They have a few intimate moments but get separated by a quirk of fate. Meanwhile, Sowcar delivers a child but goes on to become an I.A.S. officer, turning up as his boss in a collector's office where Appa is a senior clerk. By now he is married to Jayanthi, and they have a son, who becomes a friend of Sowcar's son. It was the story of a middle-class family man caught between his love for a former girlfriend (and mother of his child) and his dear wife.

K. Balachander recounts that his first meeting with Appa had left him feeling humiliated and angry. Balachander's play, *Major Chandrakanth*, had been a huge success and there was an opportunity to make it into a film. Balachander, at the suggestion of Rangarajan (of *The Hindu* newspaper group), ventured to meet Gemini and was told that he could narrate the script in the car as he was going to the airport. Though he didn't like the idea, Balachander agreed, only to find that Appa's attention span was short. He got off at the airport to meet someone and said they

A duet

Appa with Ragini, the youngest of the Travancore sisters (Lalitha, Padmini, Ragini) in the film, Ezhai Pangalan *(1963).*

could continue on the way back. Balachander left in a huff, hailing a taxi. However, the two did eventually work together, for the first time in *Iru Kodugal*, and the experience completely changed Balachander's opinion of him. He would say that Appa was a director's dream; he was like potter's clay, you could mould him into the character you had conceptualized.

K. Balachander would also point out to Appa that he was a restless person, unable to sit quietly even for a few minutes. Between shots he would buzz off from the sets, and return when his shot was due. All his friends and acquaintances were familiar with Gemini's 'restlessness'. And he would never sit on a chair the normal way; he would turn it around, and sit with his legs on either side of the backrest, his elbows on top of the back of the chair! Yet he was patience personified when he had to take a flight or train. He was always well on time, preferring to wait rather than be late. He was time-conscious when it came to appointments, shooting schedules and social functions. If he were the chief guest, you could be sure that he would never be late. He would din it into our heads that punctuality was an important virtue. 'Don't take the other person's time for granted,' he would say.

Onscreen father and son

Appa with S.V. Ranga Rao, a thespian who essayed character roles. They acted together in several films.

The 1959 film, *Kalyana Parisu* ('Wedding Gift'), directed by Sridhar, who was then probably the youngest filmmaker around, was a silver jubilee hit. It was a different kind of love triangle. Saroja Devi, the heroine, sacrifices her love for the hero when she learns that her sister loves him, too. In the end, the sister dies leaving a son behind, but it is too late for the lovers to come together again. She gets married to someone else and the hero leaves his child with her as a wedding gift. Remade in Hindi as *Nazrana*, the film had haunting songs and terrific dialogues, and then on, the actors and the director were much sought after.

Director Sridhar had to wait for Appa to get well first before signing him for *Kalyana Parisu*. Appa contracted typhoid and Sridhar was certain that he was the one. The wait was worthwhile, he said, because he knew that only Gemini could do justice to the role. Sridhar directed Appa in several films after that – *Sumaithangi* ('The One Who Bears Burdens'), *Meenda Swargam*, ('Paradise Regained'), *Then Nilavu* ('Honeymoon'), and *Avalukkendru Oru Manam*, ('She Has a Mind of Her Own') co-starring Devika, Padmini, Vyjayanti and Bharati.

I haven't really heard or seen Appa prepare for roles that came naturally to him, which were those of the romantic or the tragic hero. However, for roles that were different from his 'usual' ones, he did make a special effort. I remember him taking dancing lessons to portray Shiva in *Ganga Gauri*. The Bharatanatyam master would come home to give lessons and I would peep from the door so as not to distract them. It was fascinating to watch Appa in his tennis shorts and t-shirt doing

FACING PAGE:

Labour of love

Appa made up to essay the role of a disfigured protagonist in Kanavane Kan Kanda Deivam, *1955. Several hours were required to do the make-up and till the day's filming was complete and make-up removed, he could not eat.*

BOTTOM:

Say cheese!

R.K. Karanjia, Appa and Hemamalini at a function in the early 1970s.

intricate footwork demonstrated by the teacher. He seemed to enjoy it. As did I.

The other role he worked hard at was that of a *kurava* or gypsy that he portrayed in *Kurathi Magan* ('Gypsy's Son') with K.R. Vijaya. To prepare for the role, he spent time with the community to observe their ways, language, mannerisms and routine.

Once, Appa heard of a film being planned on the story of Victor Hugo's *The Hunchback of Notre Dame*. Eager to snag the lead role, Appa dressed for the part and went to the producer's home. Taking him for a beggar, they gave him alms and asked him to leave. They were delighted to discover his true identity and the role was given to him.

Kanavane Kankanda Deivam ('My Husband is My God') released in 1955 and was well received. Both Appa and Anjali Devi got good reviews for their performances. It's the story of a king who turns blind and needs a serpent's jewel from the netherworld to regain his vision. The hero, a palace employee who is in love with the princess, accepts the challenge to procure the jewel, which is in the custody of the serpent queen (played by Lalitha, one of the Travancore sisters – Lalitha, Padmini, Ragini). But the

LEFT:

Comrades on stage

Bollywood actor Amrish Puri with Appa at the staging of a play in Mumbai (1994-95).

BOTTOM:

Gold rush

Sivaji Ganesan, Appa holding Gigi in his arms, donating gold to the National Defence Fund, responding to the appeal of Prime Minister Lal Bahadur Shastri, who is seen receiving the ornaments.

Backstage in Mumbai

From left: Rishi Kapoor, Shatrughan Sinha, Appa, Randhir Kapoor, Shammi Kapoor and Neetu Singh in 1994-95 during the staging of a play where Appa was the sutradhar *(compere).*

serpent queen falls for the hero, and he plays along to get his hands on the jewel. When the serpent queen comes to know of his true intentions, she curses him and he turns into an ugly hunchback. Yet the princess marries him and they end up living in a hut. They have a son and the story goes on to narrate how the mother and son help the hero regain his original form, to live happily ever after.

In March, 1962, a charity Film Stars' Cricket Match was organized at the Corporation Stadium in Chennai to collect funds for the Red Crescent Hospital. It was Raj Kapoor's team versus Gemini Ganesan's team. Raj Kapoor's team members included Sivaji Ganesan, Rajendra Kumar, Nimmi, Jamuna, Shashi Kapoor, Nirupa Roy, Prem Nazir, Chandra Babu, Shyama and Johnny Walker, while Gemini Ganesan's team included Dilip Kumar, Savithri, Shammi Kapoor, Waheeda Rehman, Raaj Kumar, Ragini, I.S. Johar, Pran and Shubha Khote. I was eight years old at the time, and at the match, recollect the Telugu actress Jamuna in white trousers and shirt, dark glasses studded with white stones in keeping with the fashion of the times, and two braids doubled with red ribbons. Appa played well, hitting several sixes, and that's about all I can remember, apart from the stars flitting in and out of the pavilion where I was seated.

Then Nilavu ('Honeymoon') was shot almost entirely in Kashmir. I was in the third standard. It was school summer vacation time and Bobjima, Revathi, Kamala and I were taken to Srinagar where we stayed for three months in a rented house called 'White House'. M.N. Nambiar – who played the villain in the film – and his family were there too. His daughter, Sneha, and I would climb cherry trees and pluck the fruit and get chased by the gardener. Fed up of complaints, Appa hired one cherry tree for our exclusive use for the time we were there! The film's leading lady was Vyjayantimala, and we would often watch them shoot – on Dal Lake, at the Shalimar gardens, in Gulmarg. Savithri Aunty, as I called her, was there as well with her mother and daughter, Viji. She would come too, sometimes, for the shoot. She would swim in the lake.

Director Sridhar and his beautiful wife, Devasena, became close friends of the

State honours

Above: Appa receiving the Padmashri from President V.V. Giri in 1971. Rekha was awarded the Padmashri by President Pratibha Patil in 2010.
Below: Prime Minister Indira Gandhi, Appa and Bobjima after the National Civilian Awards ceremony (1971).

The small screen

Eighty-year-old Appa as the orthodox family patriarch in the year-long Tamil television serial, Krishnadasi, *produced by Kutty Padmini in 2000.*

family. He made *Ninaivellam Nithya* ('All My Thoughts are of Nithya') in 1982 with my younger sister, Gigi, and Karthik in lead roles. In his later years, he did not keep good health and had to use a wheelchair. That did not stop him from coming personally to wish Appa and Bobjima on their *Sadabhishekam*, Appa's eightieth birthday celebrations when they renewed their wedding vows.

In September 2000, when he turned eighty, Appa began acting in a teleserial, *Krishnadasi*, made by Kutty Padmini, the child-star of *Kuzhandiyum Deivamum* ('God and child'). He was playing the role of a family patriarch, a strict disciplinarian, who kept the family on their toes. The show received high TRP ratings and the entire cast participated in his eightieth birthday celebrations, wishing him well.

Yaar Paiyan? ('Whose Son?'), *Karpagam*, *Ramu*, *Parthal Pasi Theerum*, ('My Hunger is Appeased by Looking at You'), *Konjum Salangai* ('Endearing Anklets') and *Raj Tilak* ('Coronation') are some of my favourites among Appa's films. Well-known child-actor Daisy Irani played a little boy in *Yaar Paiyan* who follows Appa around, claiming him as his father. *Karpagam* was K.R. Vijaya's debut film, she did a great job and the two of them looked good together. Savithri, too, was in the film. *Ramu* tugged at the heartstrings, and for the most part, Appa's character in the movie is a sad and tragic one. In *Konjum Salangai* he played a nadaswaram player with two women seeking his love, Kumari Kamala and Savithri. The former is a dancer and the latter, a singer.

I confess I haven't seen all of Appa's films. I've liked almost all of what I've seen, except for a couple of (later) films where for some reason he was made to wear a wig that looks awful, like in *Annai Velanganni* with Jayalalitha. I loved his part in *Avvai Shanmugi*, especially the way he looks longingly at the nanny played by Kamal Haasan.

Revathi has the whole collection of Appa's films, earlier in videotape and now in DVDs, at her home in Peoria, Illinois. She watches some of it every day, she says, either when she is soaking in her bath after work, or on a holiday. Kamala too has taken to regularly watching Appa's films and now she knows most of them well, including songs and dialogues. Gigi, too, has a collection, not just of Appa's films but also of several candid home videos, that she is loath to share with the rest of us lest they get lost! As for me, I still cannot bring myself to watch any of his films because they remind me of him and I am saddened.

Gemini Ganesan, the actor, was best known for his good looks, charming disposition, romantic portrayals and his essaying the tragic, lovelorn hero. He was lucky that most of his films had haunting melodies and beautiful lyrics, sung by talented artistes like A.M. Raja,

Different moods

Posing to show different emotions. Appa was most comfortable essaying roles that were both romantic and tragic.

A.L. Raghavan, P.B. Srinivas and Soundararajan. They say A.M. Raja's voice matched his natural voice the best, like Mukesh's matched Raj Kapoor's.

Mythology, social drama, comedy, romance, tragedy, Appa's roles were mostly related to these; none were what are called 'action' films, nor did he do song sequences that needed extraordinary dancing abilities. Action was woven into the stories where necessary – a fencing sequence or sword fight here, a bit of a scuffle there, with the hero emerging unscathed even when attacked by a bunch of goons. The genre belonged to another era, and Appa's films and his roles are best remembered in that context.

LEFT:

Reflecting the times

Appa wearing styish reflector sunglasses that continue to be popular in Tamil Nadu. I too had a pair as a child!

BOTTOM:

All in a day's work

Left: At a colleague's house, perhaps to discuss a script. Right: Outside the sets, getting briefed on the scene that is to be filmed.

CHAPTER FOUR
The Family

The family is one of nature's masterpieces.

– George Santayana

Throughout Appa's tenure in films, his family never hosted or attended any film parties. When we were growing up, there weren't many film magazines that published gossip, or television channels that relayed news from the world of entertainment. So G.G.'s family led a fairly sheltered life, content to send its children to school and college, going about the business of running a household that included cows, dogs, rabbits, aquariums and that received scores of relatives, friends and fans every day. Annual vacations were spent mostly in the hills or on pilgrimages.

Appa had four daughters with Bobji – Revathi, Kamala, Narayani and Jayalakshmi (Gigi). Savithri, also an actor, with whom he lived for more than fifteen years – she had her own household – bore him two children: a daughter, Vijayachamundeshwari, and a son, Sathish. Gender, to Appa, seemed incidental, for he made no fuss over the fact that only one of his children was male.

Growing up, we learned that he had had two daughters with Pushpavalli, an actress and his senior, soon after I was born – Bhanurekha and Radha. Despite his stable of affairs and long, intimate relationships with other women, Bobji remained the undisputed leader of the Gemini household.

Was Appa ever disappointed that none of us were sons? The following diary entry on the day of my birth (26 December 1953) with the heading, 'Our third baby born today', lay to rest my doubts. 'Bobji delivered a baby girl at 10:05 A.M. today...Bobji and mother expected a baby boy but I like this child very much and I am sure this is going to be a 'lucky' child. May God bless her! Poor Bobji, nice girl, is very patient.' Gangamma had decided what the baby's name would be – Narayanasamy, after Appa's granduncle. When the baby turned out to be female, she simply amended the name to Narayani!

FACING PAGE:

Picture perfect

Standing left to right: Narayani, Revathi, Kamala. Seated left to right: Gangamma, Appa and Bobjima with Jaya (Gigi) on her lap (1962).

విజయ సం॥ మార్గశిర బ ౬ శనివారము.

விஜய௵ மார்கழிமீ ௧௧ உ சனிக்கிழமை.

ವಿಜಯ ಸಂ॥ ಮಾರ್ಗಶಿರ ಬ ೬ ಶನಿವಾರವು.

൧൧൨൯ ധനുമാസം ൧൧ ശനിയാഴ്ച.

شنبہ ۱۹ ویں ربیع الثانی سنہ ۱۳۷۳ *

Our third baby born today

Sow. Bobji delivered a baby girl at 10.5 AM today. Thanks to Patti the delivery was made much more easy. Bobji & mother expected a boy but I like this child very much and I am sure this is going to be a 'lucky' child! May God bless her! Poor Bobji, nice girl, is very patient.

Sow. Ambulu also gave birth to a boy at Triplicane at 9.30 AM today.

Phoned up Nelo & informed them.

Lucky child

Appa's diary entry on the day of my birth, 26 December 1953, where he also records the birth of his cousin Ambulu's second child. Gangamma had gone off to help in that delivery and could come to Bobjima's aid only later.

I remember Gangamma as always exuding positive vibrations, with a half smile on her lips, ever cheerful and friendly. Chinamma, her sister, would criticize her for being '*Aal kanda samundaram*'. That's a Tamil proverb meaning 'as gregarious as the waves of the sea that rush to the shore at the sight of visitors'. That was an apt description, for no one went away from our home without receiving at least a little bit of hospitality. This could mean a tall glass of buttermilk, coffee or Ovaltine, a bunch of freshly-plucked flowers, a clutch of greens from the kitchen garden, or homemade sweetmeats. As much as Gangamma loved entertaining visitors, Chinamma detested the thought. As her older sister got busy welcoming people into the house, Chinamma would plot and plan how to eject them as soon as possible. And so they sparred, the two sisters, much to the delight of us children; for us it was all fun and games. Appa was close to both Gangamma and Chinamma, and they in turn doted on him.

Posing together

A studio picture of my parents with Bobjima looking into the camera albeit shyly, and Appa, away!

Gangamma had no formal training in music, yet, at the first opportunity, she would break into song. And she was a wizard in the kitchen. Did she go to school? 'Yes, till the fifth standard,' she would say, chuckling. 'It rained one day and then I just refused to go after that.'

Gangamma, and my mother, were from a generation that believed in conservation. Gangamma would collect used envelopes and turn them inside out for reuse. She meticulously rolled on empty spools threads from rose garlands that Appa would bring home from public functions. The fragrant *desi* rose petals, a fetching pink, were carefully collected and made into delicious *gulkand* (sweet rose chutney). When Appa encouraged Bobjima to enroll for Hindi classes at the Hindi Prachar Sabha in Chennai, she used the blank side of Appa's old Chemistry practical books to make her notes. In the margins she would write her *dhobi* lists and grocery lists.

Gangamma was ninety-seven when she died in Chennai, with the entire family (except Revathi) – daughter-in-law, grandchildren and great-grandchildren – crowding around her, holding her hand, stroking her, talking to her. Only her beloved son was missing – he was away shooting and by the time he came, she was gone. What were her last words? 'Has Ganesan eaten?'

Family portrait

Left to right: Narayani, Bobjima, Appa with his hands resting on Gigi's shoulders. A studio photo clicked in T. Nagar, Chennai while I was an undergraduate student at Stella Maris College and Gigi was at school at Presentation Convent.

Appa would say that his mother was the most patient and good-natured person he ever knew. She rarely lost her composure, even in the most trying of times. In December 1964, Appa had gone to Rameswaram and Dhanushkodi – a town on its eastern tip, south east of Pamban and only fifteen kilometers from Sri Lanka – with our family doctor-couple, Ramakrishnan and Jayam. Savithri accompanied him, probably pregnant with their son, Sathish. I think it was a kind of a pilgrimage, for the places on their itinerary were of religious significance and visiting them is considered as fulfilling as making a trip to Kashi. Dhanushkodi means 'bow's end', a reference to Rama's bow.

One morning the front pages of all newspapers splashed reports of an unexpected cyclone, with twenty-foot high tidal waves, devastating Dhanushkodi in the dead of night on December 22, taking everything with it. The waves had washed away everything; trains were derailed, houses smashed and only dead bodies and debris were left. The headlines asked, 'Where are Gemini Ganesan and Savithri?'

We panicked. Were they safe? All communication systems had been swept away; there were no means of contact. Mahalingam rushed to Mandapam, the closest point. Still, there was no news. Anxious queries and condolence messages started pouring in. Gangamma just sat like the Buddha, eyes closed, rolling her prayer beads and chanting. Actor Muthuraman came calling first thing in the morning. I vividly remember his holy ash-smeared forehead and crisp, white shirt and *dhoti* as he sat gently on the large wooden swing in the hall downstairs, head bowed.

'I am so sorry,' he began, in a voice choked with emotion. 'Oh, don't be sorry,' said Gangamma, opening her eyes. 'He'll be back.' And she resumed her prayerful chanting. After a while, Muthuraman left, and I ran to tell the others what had transpired. The flame of hope suddenly glowed brighter. And righty-ho, back he was, with Savithri, friends and all. They were to stay overnight at Dhanushkodi, but Appa changed his mind and insisted they move on. And so they lived to tell the amazing story of how unknowingly, they had been one step ahead of the cyclone. Since all the railway lines got wrenched off, there is now no train to Dhanushkodi. The ravaged place was declared a 'ghost town' by the state government and so it remains, to this day.

Turn it around

This was how Appa would sit on a chair at the studios and also at home. He would simply turn the chair around and let his legs hang on either side of the backrest.

Did Gangamma whoop with joy at her only child's safe return? No. She smiled broadly and continued with her routine while we children showered Appa with questions and love, touching him, hugging him, grateful that he'd come back alive. And Bobjima? She must have been hovering in the background, shy and diffident; I don't remember now.

Revathi and Kamala say they had a wonderful time with Appa and Bobji in their years growing up in Madras. Appa would personally choose their

Up in the air

Revathi holding Jaya (Gigi) up in the air – something all the children in Gemini households were used to.

clothes and jewelry in the evening, comb their hair and apply *kaajal* (kohl) to their eyes, even painting their nails with Cutex (as nail polish was called then) before the family set off for Marina beach. It was an almost daily outing that they eagerly looked forward to. He would buy them ice cream and chocolates on demand (the children would whisper their wish-list into his ear) and spend time chatting on the sands.

Revathi, the first-born, was his special child and also Gangamma's, who practically raised her, and Kamala was my mother's. Revathi was frail and needed extra attention and special diets, while Kamala was the rebel, the naughty one who would turn up with scraped knee and elbow. When clothes had to be bought, Appa would insist they were well-coordinated – most times they wore identical clothes and jewelry, 'almost as though we were going to a wedding,' Revathi recollects. Shopping was a delightful ritual, picking and choosing, buying the best. When they graduated to wearing saris, the store trips continued, with him buying them similar saris in maybe different colours. Long years later, I made twin quilts with two of their identical 'butter-nylex' saris that he'd brought back from a trip to Ceylon.

I was born ten years after Revathi and nine years after Kamala. Jayalakshmi was born eight years after me. I was suspended in the middle, as it were, left to my own resources for entertainment and company. That probably explains why I ended up playing many a times at Savithri Aunty's house with Viji, her daughter, who was five years my junior. I was also the recipient of many a thrashing and scolding from my mother, since the older sisters were away and the youngest was yet a baby. Bobjima must have gone through a great deal, and she vented all that on me whenever I gave her the chance! I loved her dearly, though I feared her bouts of temper. If I tried to complain about her to Gangamma and Chinamma, I would be told off roundly and they would ask me to be patient and understanding. 'Poor Bobji,' they would chorus.

On birthdays, Appa took special care to gift us books that would last, mostly reference books. On her fourteenth birthday, he presented Revathi with a complete set of the Encyclopedia Britannica. How excited we were! It occupied pride of place in a glass cupboard in the living room. Earlier, on her twelfth birthday, he had bought Revathi a piano as she was taking piano lessons. She went on to qualify in the Trinity College of Music, London, senior level examinations, both theory and practice.

Making music

Revathi and Kamala giving a veena recital at a function organized by the Lions Club, Madras, to raise funds for a social cause.

Another fond childhood memory is of the scrumptious cakes that Appa would get us from McRennets, a bakery-cum-confectionery store on Mount Road. Sometimes when he dropped me off at school in the morning before proceeding to the studios, he would stop by at McRennets and buy me my favourite bun stuffed with butter and jam. We all remember the Japanese cream cakes he would get from there, creamy and delicious.

Most birthdays he would take me to Higginbotham's, the legendary bookstore on Mount Road, and let me loose. 'Choose whatever you want to read,' he would say, winking at me. And he would proceed to chat with the staff and other shoppers, or browse through the sections. A friend from Higginbotham's, Chandrasekhar, fondly remembers those visits and his New Year ritual of buying Hoe & Co. diaries for himself, family and friends. He would write a New Year message on the first page and sign off with a flourish.

None of us were consistent at keeping diaries. Even the few we kept had mundane entries like, 'I woke up at six A.M.,' or 'went to sleep at nine P.M.'. Maybe we were fearful that Bobjima might read our secret thoughts and dreams and haul us over the coals! I had the Junior Science Encyclopedia volumes that Appa gave me one birthday, with colourful illustrations and diagrams. Jaya, as a child, scribbled on all of them and I was furious at the desecration of my prized possession.

While Revathi was studious and obediently practised the piano and veena, Kamala was more inclined towards drawing and painting. She

From a father to a daughter

Appa writing to Revathi who had moved to the U.S. Appa would type out letters on his Remington typewriter, usually using just the right hand index finger. While storing it away, he would always leave a blank sheet in the roller, saying he was instructed to do so while buying it. After he passed away, we found the typewriter with a blank sheet of paper intact in the roller.

Gemini Ganesh

PHONE: 84630
2 A, NUNGAMBAKKAM HIGH ROAD
MADRAS-34

3.8.1972

My dear child Revathi,

I am writing this letter particularly to you. I have been noting a note homesickness in all your letters. It is a real sickness without which only your body and mind could be healthy.

When I was thirteen I was sent to study at Ramakrishna Mission Students Home, Mylapore. I had to be away from home and mother for one year. I never seperated myself from amma even while sleeping and I felt like Robinson Crusoe on a desert island. I used to write letters every week expressing my loneliness, homesickness and how I wished to die!

Just imagine; for all these letters, I did not get a single reply from Amma! She always beleived in the Divinity that shapes our ends rough hew it how we will! She strongly beleived that I should find the 'home' wherever I went and stayed and I should develop the sense of adaptibility.

In these days of struggle for existence, it is but natural that parents want their children to live well and better. Conditions here are not very favourable for an ambitious individual. Your husband is not the असत्यमेव जयते hypocritical, selfish, egotistic, pecuniary, time serving type to suceed materially in future down here. Also as an accomplished doctor, wife and mother I want you to have a change for the better in a new world where umpteen vistas are open for expansion of human capacities, and ambitious enterprises.

As such I have told you times without number that you should give time and tide a change to improve things for the better and that you should try your best to live well there and pursue your carrer there in the best manner possible.

Do you think that we do not miss you or is there a moment when we so not think of you? We also feel sick that you are not with us. Should I write and tell you how Doctor and Akka miss you! Our lives are almost over but we will never say die! We want you to live much better than us and we want you all to be the shining exemplars to the youth of India.

I am sure after a few weeks you are defenitely going to feel much, much better and a trip that one of us might take there in the near future may make you rejuvenated. Please find enclosed a cheque.

With best wishes and love to Amu, and Rajesh,

Your loving father

GG

made a charcoal portrait of Appa while she was at medical school. Her sketches of deities like Brahma and Ganesha hang on the walls at our Kodaikanal home, Redlynch. She has painted several saris for me with flowers and other motifs. She was also good at baking cakes. Both Kamala and Revathi took veena lessons. I was made to learn Carnatic vocal music when I refused to continue with veena lessons (the teacher, Ranganayaki, would rap your knuckles with a foot ruler when you made mistakes). I enjoyed learning to play the piano.

When Revathi and Kamala chose to study medicine, Appa was delighted. Despite getting very good grades, the girls had to seek admission in a private medical college in Manipal, Karnataka, because of a quota system in Tamil Nadu that did not favour students from the 'forward classes'.

Revathi says she saw Appa cry for the first time when he realized that they would be separated by hundreds of miles. He escorted them to college personally, saw to all the admission formalities and, I remember, charmed the entire faculty, students and head of the Kasturba Medical

Smiles 'n saris

The four sisters standing in reverse order – youngest to oldest, from left to right – at a family function in Chennai. The Kancheevaram saris are similar but of different colours this time.

BOTTOM:

First wedding among sisters

Revathi and Swaminathan (Amu) at their wedding on 5 May 1968. Sowcar Janaki is seen handing them a gift and Appa is standing next to her.

RIGHT:

Decades later...

Appa visiting Revathi and Amu in the U.S. Here he is being shown around a medical centre in Peoria, Illinois, the town where the couple made their home.

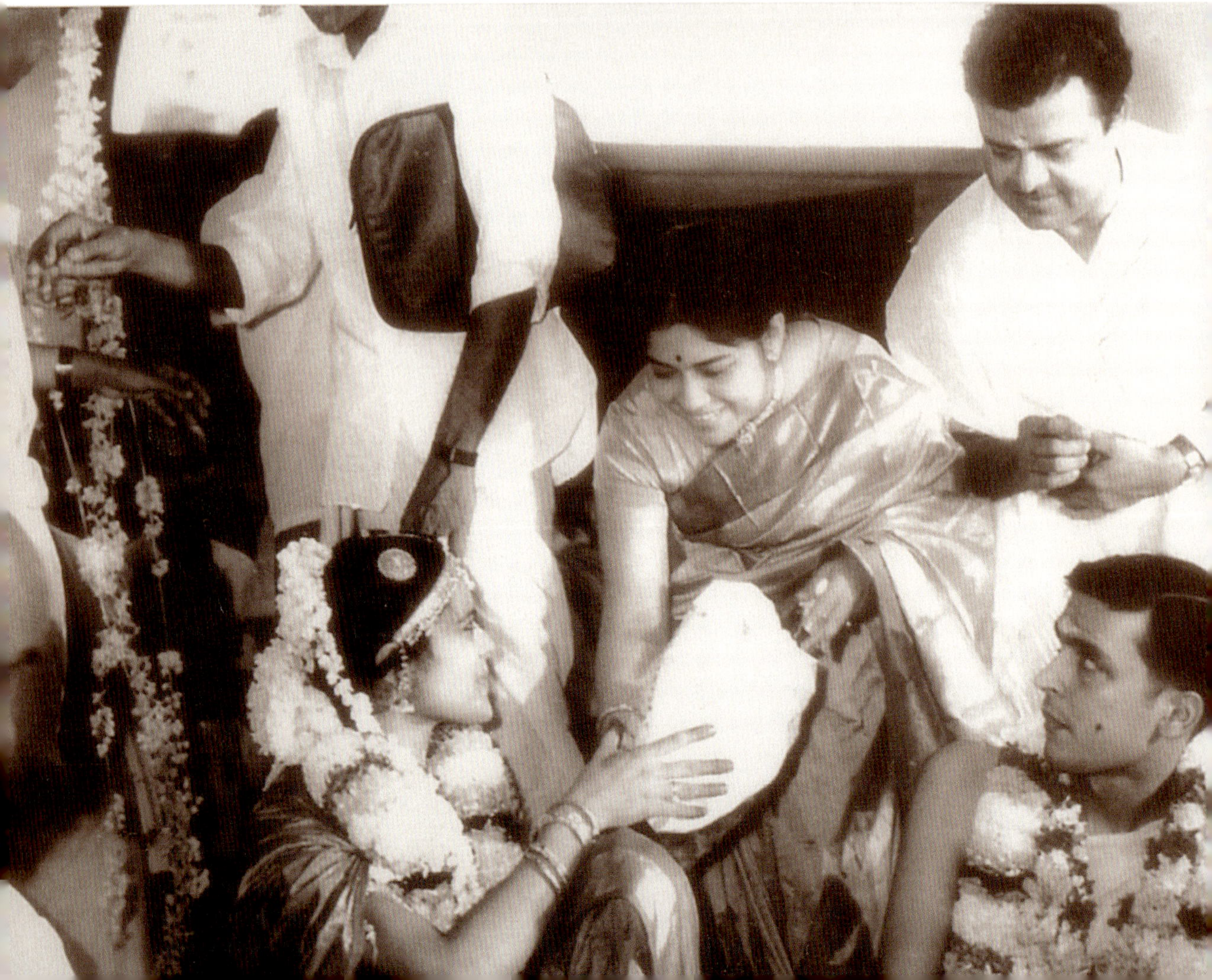

The invitation

The simple wedding invitation card giving details of the marriage ceremony that was held at the Abbotsbury Hall in Chennai. Hemamalini gave a classical dance performance at the reception. She was just beginning her career then as a film actress.

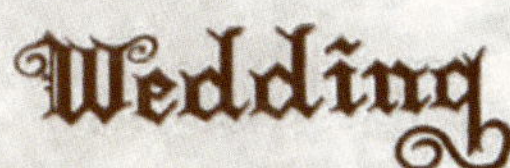

5-5-1968

Sow. Revathi, M.B., B.S.,

Chi. Swaminathan, M.B.,B.S.,

Programme

*

MUHURTHAM : 5-5-1968 ... 6.30 to 7.15 a.m.

NADHASWARAM

Thiruvaduthurai Aadhina Vidhwan 'Nadhaswararathinam'
Thiruvizhimizhalai S. Govindarajan brothers

THAVUL

'Layagnana Karpanai Kalanidhi'
Vadapathimangalam G. Dakshinamurthy &
Nachiarkoil 'Layagnanamani' T. Chelliah

RECEPTION : 5-5-1968

BHARATHANATYAM ... 6.05 p.m.

'Nruthyajyothi' Kumari Hemamalini

CLARIONET ... 8 p. m.

Thiruvaduthurai Aadhina Vidhwan
Tiruchi A. K. C. Natarajan and Party

Sri Gemini Ganesh

and

Smt. Bobji Ganesh

request the pleasure of your company

on the occasion of the marriage

of their eldest daughter

Sow. Revathi, M.B., B.S.,

with

Chi. Swaminathan, M.B.,B.S.,
Son of Dr. S. Rajagopalan
and
Dr. Mrs. Shanthasundari, Madras-17.

on Sunday, May 5th, 1968

at "Abbotsbury" Mount Road, Madras

With the best compliments of:

Smt. Savithri Ganesh

New age wedding

At the wedding of Kamala and Selvaraj on 7 September 1971. Left to right: Appa, his manager V. Mahalingam, Madhavan, M. Karunanidhi, Selvaraj and Kamala.

College. He visited them whenever he could. Once he drove to Manipal with Bobjima in their new Standard Herald car. In the morning, they found the car missing. Four engineering students had picked the locks and taken the car for a joyride, but had got involved in an accident and the car lay crumpled on the highway, like a piece of crushed paper. The furious principal rusticated the students. Later, when the students' parents wrote to Appa, he requested the college to pardon them and take them back as it would affect their future.

Appa was mighty proud of his girls. He encouraged all of us to study well, though by the time I grew up, he had no time to pay personal attention to my studies like he had done with Revathi and Kamala. I remember once we were being introduced to visitors by Appa. 'This is Revathi, my first daughter, and she is studying medicine. Kamala, my second, also studying medicine. And this is the third, Narayani...' He turned to me, 'Tell uncle which class you are studying in?'

Though he did sit me down one day, when after completing a B.A. in Economics from Stella Maris College, Chennai, I was confused as to what I should do next. I definitely wasn't interested in medicine; at least I wasn't inclined to become a medical professional. I wasn't brave enough, I thought, to take decisions and tend to people suffering physical pain.

When I filled out forms to apply for law school, Bobjima protested. 'Bad choice,' she scolded. Ditto when I wished to apply for flying lessons.

Appa's advice to me was that there are only two great professions in the world – one was medicine, because you could heal people and there would always be people who needed to get well. The other, he said, was teaching because everyone needed guidance to gain knowledge and skills. And, he added, triumphantly, 'They're both gratifying professions. Patients and students never forget a good doctor or teacher.' And why didn't he become either a doctor or a teacher? 'Ah, well,' he said, 'I didn't have the opportunity then. Moreover, as an actor, I have the privilege of being a doctor, teacher, engineer, plumber, singer, anything. Isn't that wonderful?'

When her mother, Savithri, married off Vijayachamundeshwari, still in her teens, Appa was livid. The long-time relationship between him and Savithri had broken down, and at the time of Viji's wedding – arranged to a relative, Govind Rao, a bank employee – Appa was touring abroad. Education was something Appa valued greatly, and he would often emphasize the virtues of a good college education and choice of career. 'You should be equipped with specialized knowledge and be able to stand on your own feet,' he would say. A few years later, after Viji's first son was born, he encouraged her to enroll in a women's college from where she graduated in English Literature.

Etched in memory

A charcoal sketch that Kamala made of Appa while she was a student at medical school, where she took art lessons as a hobby, encouraged by Appa who used to sketch and paint a lot as a student.

The first time I saw Appa get very emotional was the night Revathi got married. We came home after the reception and Bobjima, Appa and I were in the bedroom that was full of wedding knick-knacks. Bobjima was seated on the bed. Suddenly Appa came from the bathroom, knelt in front of her, buried his head in her lap and cried loudly. We were stunned. What happened? 'My child has gone away,' he said, between sobs. 'How will I live without her?'

Revathi was as attached to Appa as he was to her. Her husband, Swaminathan, was a doctor too; post-M.B.B.S. he'd done a course in dermatology and she, in obstetrics and gynaecology. Her mother-in-law, Shantasundari, was a renowned obstetrician-gynaecologist and her father-in-law, Rajagopalan, a popular dermatologist. Her married home

was in Mambalam, T.Nagar, at Masilamani Street, just a few kilometers from our home in Nungambakkam, and we would visit her every evening. She worked in the Family Planning Centre of the Government Women and Children's Hospital at Egmore, and would stop by our house every morning on her way to work. Ironically, it was the child closest to him who would move thousands of miles away to the U.S. to do her residency, after she and Swaminathan failed to secure admission in the post-graduate degree courses of their choice in Madras. Both had stood first in their respective diploma courses.

Maybe it is all for the good, Appa would say, because Revathi switched her specialization to radiation oncology after taking a couple of years off to care for her son, who was three years old when they arrived in the U.S. Sensitive by nature, Revathi fainted the first time she was to assist in delivering a baby. However, in the decades she has been a radiation oncologist, patients have adored the same sensitivity in her as she empathizes with and understands their emotional state. She is probably the most soft-spoken and gentlest of all the siblings, with deep family ties.

Kamala's relationship with Appa was very different from any of us, on account of the peculiar circumstances that forced her to protect and mother him during a difficult period in his life. After he and Savithri got estranged and separated, he took to the bottle to drown his sorrows, and it was left to Kamala to answer distress calls from his friends who would ask for someone to come and collect him. She would drive off, sometimes late into the night, with a chowkidar or a gardener in tow, looking for her father and ministering to him, coaxing him to come home. Not an enviable duty. While she was out, Bobjima and the two grandmothers would pace up and down, praying that he was well, and that Kamala was safe, and heave a sigh of relief once Kamala brought him home.

During this period, whenever I felt Kamala was being harsh with Appa, scolding him or telling him off for not being more responsible and dignified, I would rush to his defence. My heart ached for him. Kamala would flare up, 'Have you ever been faced with the humiliating prospect of collecting an inebriated father from someone's house?' And I would shut up, not knowing what else to do. She has, on many occasions, stood with her arms stretched out, blocking his way as he revved up the car engine to go out for a drink late at night. Kamala was young and vulnerable, too, but was spunky enough to handle the situation the best way she could, in a household of bewildered women who had no idea how to deal with Appa's dejection.

Appa did come out of that period of sadness, somewhat. He had responsibilities, work, the rest of his family, and how much they loved and cared for him! However, there were anxious moments – what if he was offered drinks at a social occasion or at a friend's place? Sometimes it did happen and there were a few worrying moments, but there was nothing that could not be handled by the band of brave women at home.

When Kamala stubbornly insisted that she would marry Dr Francis Victor Selvaraj – son of Dr Somaiah, who had converted to Christianity, and his Protestant wife, Navaneethammal – my father remained composed while my mother was inconsolable. Kamala and Selvaraj married in an unorthodox function, presided over by M. Karunanidhi and other social reform activists. It was what was then called an 'inter-caste, inter-faith marriage'. And it made waves in our community. Which is why, though I was barely eighteen at the time, my mother got busy scouting a match for me.

Come what may, Bobjima's faith in the *shruti-smriti samskara* (Indic tradition and culture) remained unshaken. She continued, till the very end, to be an avid temple-goer, and was prayerful in everything she did. Her interest in spirituality, philosophy and science never waned. She did mellow a great deal with age and the experiences of her children and grandchildren. What was unacceptable to her a few decades ago, she gracefully absorbed later as an inevitable part of the changing times. Appa, however, remained an enigma – I never could fathom what he thought of faith and religion, per se. I think he liked to know of these things but wasn't too sure himself if he should get too involved in them. That's the

TOP FACING PAGE:

Peas in a pod

Kamala, me, Appa, Revathi and Gigi posing in front of the teakwood temple at my parents' home in Nungambakkam, Chennai. Again, the sisters are wearing identical saris! On the wall hangs an original Thanjavur painting of Krishna holding up Govardhana mountain with his little finger.

BOTTOM FACING PAGE:

Eating in a row

The four sisters seated on the floor and eating off banana leaves in a traditional Tamil style meal at Revathi's house in Chennai on the day we celebrated Appa's eightieth birthday on 30 November 2000.

charm of elective faith – you can choose to believe or not to believe, even be a part-time believer, it does not shackle you.

Selvaraj was chief medical officer in the government hospital where Kamala was training. He was full of wit and humour, and the fact that he belonged to a different religion, caste and community did not deter Kamala. Gangamma and Chinamma, who on knowing that this was what Kamala wished for, gave their blessings after their initial reluctance. Appa was cordiality personified when Selvaraj's parents came to meet the family. And so they were married, in an unconventional way, in a politically-correct civil ceremony shorn of traditional ceremonies and chants, on 7 September 1971. Appa hosted a reception for them at a marriage hall in Madras.

When Kamala moved to rented accommodation after her marriage, there was a pall of gloom. Bobjima swore she would never see her again – though it was she who directed Appa's assistant, Parthasarathi, and me to go and decorate her bed with flowers, arrange jars of provisions for a month in her kitchen, and fix a mirror on the wall.

At Bobjima's insistence, my marriage was arranged in a traditional fashion to a medical doctor who worked in the United Kingdom. Appa checked with me several times if I was fine with it. I was in the first year of an M.A. degree course in Economics, and had no intention of marrying so early. 'Why, do you have a boy in mind?' thundered my mother, and I fell silent. There was no boyfriend; I just didn't wish to marry. But who was to argue with her? And so I moved to England and the next year, a baby girl was born in June 1974.

I had come to Madras for the delivery and the events that unfolded later led to a divorce and my moving back to my parents' home with my child. Back to college I went, completing the M.A. I had left halfway, and began preparing for the civil services exams, something that appealed to Bobjima. She was saddened by what had happened, and was shocked that I had agreed to a divorce. 'Why couldn't you just wait here, learning music and studying, till things got sorted out?' she asked, little knowing that in a changing world such an attitude was no longer feasible.

Kamala and my friends asked me later why I didn't put my foot down when the marriage was being arranged. I was not used to asserting myself then; I had been a compliant child and was terrified of what my mother might do if I said 'no' to her. Would she hate me? Would she go on a hunger strike? And Appa? Well, he did ask me several times if I was fine with the proposal, and all I did was shake my head in a way that meant neither 'yes' nor 'no'. When I finally plucked up the courage to say I did not wish to marry, it was too late.

At home with Tipsy

Appa and I with Tipsy, the moody spitz, he so loved in my home in Delhi. Appa was visiting me with Bobjima in 1995.

Soon, however, it was love at first sight. And another marriage, this time with a classmate from the I.A.S. tutorial where we attended coaching classes. I embarked on a new life in a new place, in Patiala, where my husband, working with a multinational corporation, was posted as field officer. Another baby girl was born in March 1981.

After her tumultuous wedding, Kamala and Bobjima didn't see or speak to each other till Kamala's son, Deepu, was born the year following her marriage, on 7 November 1972. It was the grandmothers who attended to Kamala's delivery and after; they were so loving and accepting.

As for Appa, Kamala relates of a long impasse till she got a message one day that said, 'Doctor Amma's father is no more.' Rushing on the motorbike with her husband to our home, she found everything quiet and Appa seated with his head resting on the office table, telephone in hand, in an obviously inebriated state. The two hugged each other and cried. It was his birthday. Kamala would draw or paint greetings cards for family members' birthdays and anniversaries. I remember the card she sent from Manipal on Appa and Bobjima's twenty-fifth wedding anniversary. It had the number twenty-five in silver on the front, and when you opened it,

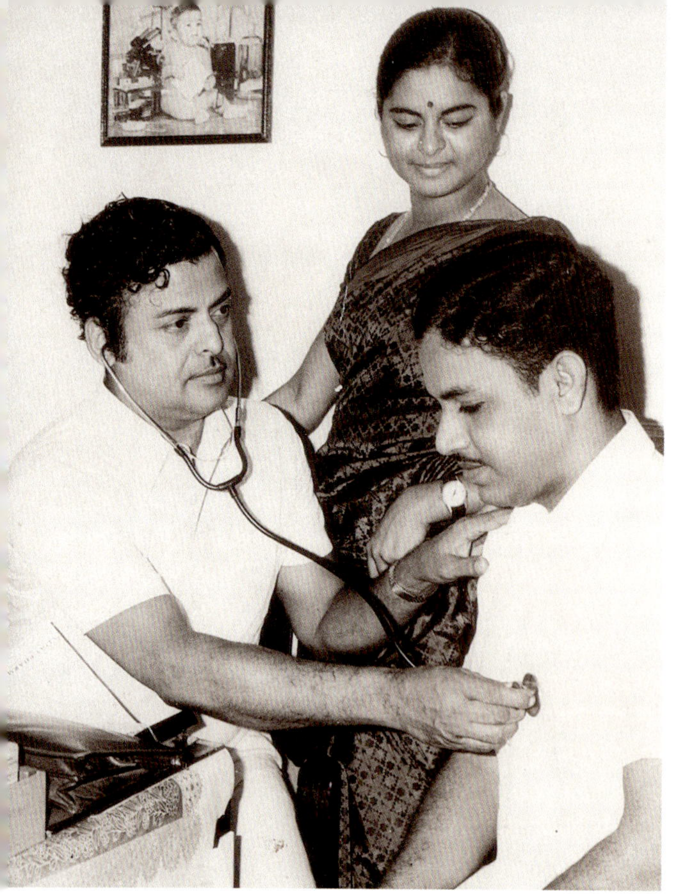

A heartbeat away

Appa listening to Selvaraj's heartbeat in their clinic during the early days of their medical practice, as Kamala looks on fondly.

the contours formed the shape of a heart. This time Appa had not heard from her and hence the call.

Then followed regular morning walks together on the beach and a sustained routine of camaraderie. Soon, Kamala and her husband moved to the first house Appa had purchased in Madras, in Nungambakkam, and this is their home to this day. Kamala and Appa began attending functions and social events together, and had ample occasion to bond as father and daughter.

Kamala and Appa also had a lot of arguments, mostly over his health and the way he had let himself go. She became the motivator, in a reversal of roles, and egged him on to accept character roles in films that came his way. She also encouraged him to do the television serial that had a one-year successful run. It was Kamala who kept alive his contacts in the film world, also perhaps because many of them came to her as patients. Kamala loved the excitement of the tinsel world and would make it a point to attend all the film awards functions and parties, with or without Appa.

She made going to Palmgrove Hotel in Nungambakkam a regular Sunday morning ritual. Mostly it was Appa and her; they would eat breakfast, enjoying the idlis, dosas and pongals, the milkshakes and coffees. Bobjima would go rarely; she would ask for a vada to be packed for her once they'd eaten. Kamala continues the tradition to this day; though our parents are no longer with us, she takes along other family members and friends, and whenever Revathi and I visit Chennai, as Madras is now called, we look forward to breakfast at Palmgrove's.

By 1994, my second marriage was on the rocks. I had by then moved to Delhi, where Appa had come to act in an English play sponsored by Unesco. He was then in good health and humour; he enjoyed his time in Delhi tremendously till he got to know about my problems towards the end of his stay. He was crushed, but tried not to show it.

'Should I come to Chennai with the children to live and work there?' I asked him, though I was happy with my job and friends in Delhi. 'Don't be silly,' he said. 'If your marriage is over, that's really too bad, but that doesn't mean you have to give up everything else. You will stay on in Delhi

Pioneering test-tube baby

Kamala with an eighteen year-old Kamalaratnam (named after her), India's second test-tube baby, born to Kamala's patients in 1990.

and carve out a happy career and life for yourself. You don't have to divorce yourself from everything.' And so he helped me buy a new home, and later, with Amma, came and spent some time with me. They made a few trips to Delhi over the years until their age and health did not permit them to travel.

Appa's proudest moment as far as Kamala is concerned came when a patient of hers, who was also Appa's long-time fan, delivered India's second test-tube baby and south India's first. Kamala never looked back; the hospital she built with great interest and devotion, G.G. Hospital, stands on the land that was part of the family's large Nungambakkam estate, just behind Appa and Bobji's home, and the houses given by Appa to Revathi and myself. Our parental home is now Jaya's, where she lives with her husband, Shreedhar, and daughter, Ganga.

On 23 February 1962, Revathi wrote in her diary, 'At 3:35 my sister was born. I went to see her at four o'clock and came back and tried to concentrate on my lessons. I just couldn't do it.' The Hollywood film *Gigi* was playing in a movie hall at the time and Revathi began to call the new baby 'Gigi'. The name stuck, though the formal name given to her was Jayalakshmi.

There was an eighteen-year gap between Revathi and Gigi; she was the baby of the family. She belonged to a new generation. Bobjima never allowed me to wear western clothes after I had attained puberty. I was always in a half-sari or sari from the age of fifteen. But with Gigi things were different. She lounged around in shorts even in her teens. I would envy her freedom to wear what she wanted, and the indulgence, the lenience. But, then, times had changed.

Married once again!

During Appa's eightieth birthday celebration and renewal of marriage vows, at Revathi's house in Chennai where Appa spent his last days with Bobjima. Kamala and her family too lived there for a few years while their house was getting renovated.

Gigi was a confidante to all our children – Revathi's son, Rajesh, Kamala's children, Deepu and Priya, and my daughters, Maya and Sonali. She would babysit the entire brood of naughty children with ease. She was closer to them in years and gave them liberties we wouldn't, and they all loved her dearly. Gigi was a favourite with Appa and Bobji, and Chinamma, who would follow her around with food, imploring her to eat.

Gigi married Shreedhar while she was in medical school. He is a writer and filmmaker who had received a national award for the best first film of a director from the Government of India in 1983 for his politically-themed film, *Kann Sivanthal Mann Sivakkum* ('Hangmen's Hymns'). They have a daughter – Ganga.

When I began writing, Appa would tell everyone, much to my embarrassment, 'You know, Narayani writes so well. She has taken after me.' Appa was a voracious reader in his younger days and he encouraged the habit in all of us. For Bobjima, too, her greatest passion was reading. She would get so carried away with a book she was reading that she would continue to read even during mealtimes, but would warn us sternly that we were not permitted to follow her example!

Appa's large book collection – we still have books he'd bought at second-hand bookshops as a college student – is wide-ranging and eclectic. There's plenty of mystery, murder, biography, autobiography, plays, cinema, science, geography, poetry, philosophy, humour, religion, sports, palmistry, astrology, crosswords, comics, encyclopedias, atlases, but strangely, not much romance! Our house at Nungambakkam was always littered with books, magazines and other reading material. Appa's collection of *Life* magazines would be stacked neatly in a glass cupboard alongside copies of *The National Geographic* and *The Illustrated Weekly of India*. I've often seen him thumb through old issues. You had to ask permission to unlock the cupboard to access those copies.

Hitting half century

Bobjima and Revathi celebrating in Peoria, U.S, when Revathi turned fifty.

In the evening of their lives, it was Kamala who took care of Appa and Bobjima, both in terms of arranging the best medical care as well as spending time with them. It was also because she was physically present there, in Chennai, while Revathi was far away in the U.S. But the two would be sent off to Revathi for long stays when Kamala got too busy or annoyed with them for not listening to her on health matters. Bobjima was asthmatic but would secretly eat sour things like pickles and raw mangoes that would aggravate her breathing problem. Appa would trouble her by refusing to bathe or not eating his medicines. If Revathi by destiny got less time to spend with her parents, she made up for it when they visited her at her home.

Appa and Bobjima's relationship, too, evolved with time. He loved her, and she him. But when they argued over something – which was a common occurrence in later years, before they grew old – he would yell at her, and she at him. Bobji was so loyal and devoted, perhaps because she didn't know otherwise, and the fact that he could not fault her irked him, especially since he was ridden with guilt over his relationships outside marriage. Bobji too lost no opportunity in riling him about his various 'misdeeds', though not explicitly. If you thought with such open exchanges you could get in a word and criticize Appa, you couldn't be more wrong. Bobjima would spring to his defence and silence you with one searing look, which meant, 'Shut up and mind your own business.'

LEFT:

Greatest Great Grand Dad

Appa and Bobjima. He is wearing a t-shirt I got for him that says, 'World's Greatest Great Grand Dad', when his first great-grandchild Selina was born to Rajesh and Geeta, Revathi's son and his wife, in the US. Next to it is a photograph of Selina, Appa and Sohaan, his great-grandchildren, on the swing at Revathi's house in Dr Thirumurthy Nagar.

TOP:

All together

At Deepu's wedding reception in Chennai, 1999. Left to right: Sathish, his wife Prasanna, Viji, Dhanalakshmi, Rekha, Kamala, Appa, Gigi and I. Seated below is Priya, Kamala's daughter.

FACING PAGE BOTTOM:

The 'Delhi family'

Standing: My older daughter, Maya. Seated left to right: Sonali, my younger daughter, myself, Bobjima and Appa, when they visited us in Delhi in the late 1980s.

Bobjima was a spirited woman; her demure appearance could be misleading. In fact it was her determination, resolve and creative entrepreneurship that kept the family together, despite Appa's many indiscretions and unforeseen financial difficulties in later years. She encountered every storm with fortitude, and found release in diverse interests like gardening, cattle rearing, pets (dogs, rabbits, fish), doll-making, weaving handbags with plastic strips, embroidery, music, and reciting from the *Vishnu Sahasranamam*, *Lalita Sahasranamam* and the Bhagavad Gita. She loved traveling to new places and had been on every pilgrimage you could think of with her friends. She so wished to go to Mount Kailash, but that was not to be. She was asthmatic, and related complications finally ended her life when she was eighty.

She was also keenly interested in science and spirituality, and would sometimes try to explain to me the similarities between the pattern of atoms and the entire universe. Then, I was a disinterested listener. Little did I know that one day I would delve deeper into them as editor of columns on those subjects.

When Appa and Bobji completed fifty years together on 30 June 1990, Kamala and Revathi organized a bash at Hotel Savera in Chennai, where they were garlanded and feted like newlyweds. Friends and relatives wished

We've done it again

Bobjima and Appa going through their marriage ceremony once again on the occasion of his eightieth birthday in Chennai. That's me behind Appa.

them well and they glowed, happy to see all their children and grandchildren around them. When Appa turned eighty, there was a family reunion and celebration, with them re-enacting their marriage vows as per custom, on 30 November 2000 at the Kalaignar Arangam, Chennai. Our parents were thrilled to bits though they said we shouldn't have made such a fuss!

When Kamala's son, Deepu, married and moved out, Appa expressed his wish to stay in his room. By now Kamala had shifted to what was then Revathi's house, close to the hospital, while her own house was undergoing renovation and repair. Appa moved into the house he'd built for Revathi, and this is where he was till the end. Bobjima was close by, at the hospital, in a room on the second floor, as she required constant monitoring for her asthma attacks. Sometimes he would go over to her room and nap there, or eat from the tiffin carrier the food Gigi would send for Amma.

When Appa and Bobji's grandchildren had begun to talk, they called Appa 'Appakutty' ('little Appa'), while Bobjima was Bobjima to all.

After the family attended Revathi's son Rajesh's wedding to Geeta in the U.S. on May 24, 1992, we spent some time together at her home in Peoria, Illinois, and travelled together to Florida, Disneyland, and other places before returning to India. Rajesh and Geeta now have three children, Selina, Sohaan and Sohil, and live in St Louis.

When I first shifted to Delhi and wished to buy myself a moped, Appa was paranoid. 'No!' he exclaimed. 'It is dangerous. Wait till you get a car. Go by bus till then.' I wonder what he would have thought of my daughter Maya's passion for motor-biking. She is a copywriter in Chennai and an avid motorcycle enthusiast. Sonali, my second daughter, has followed in the footsteps of her aunts and is a medical graduate.

The last time Appa, or rather, Appakutty, actively participated in a family function was at Kamala's daughter Priya's wedding. A little dance party was organized at her in-law's place in Chennai. When the youngsters were dancing and singing, Appa surprised everyone by shaking a leg at their request. Priya married Sanjay on 4 November 2001. In a few days, on 17 November, Appakutty turned eighty-one. Priya and Sanjay have three children, Neharikka, Lakshan and Samiksha.

It often seemed to me that Appa and Bobjima shared a sibling-like closeness–they had grown up together since their teenage years, weathered storms and raised children, each in pursuit of individual interests, with a strong matriarchal flavour provided by grandmother and grandaunt. We were a family of women, strong and self-motivated, stubborn and individualistic, soft and submissive, closely-bonded yet detached. We were an enigma to outsiders.

Appa and Bobji would consult each other and talk about their children's education, their relationships, marriages and future. Each time we found ourselves in a situation that was not easy, they were always there to support and guide us the best way they could. All the grandchildren were close to them and have many fond memories of the time they spent with them. And for that we are thankful.

Rainbow family

Standing left to right: Abu, Sonali, Dhanalakshmi, Priya and Radha. Bobjima and Appa are seated on chairs. Seated on the floor left to right: Viji, Rekha, Revathi, Kamala and I.

CHAPTER FIVE
'King of Romance'

While we look to the dramatist to give romance to realism, we ask of the actor to give realism to romance.

– Oscar Wilde

At Presentation Convent, Madras, where I studied, a girl struck up a conversation with me after school one day. I must have been nine or ten years old. 'Why do you and your sister go home in different cars?' she asked. I was puzzled. My two older sisters had finished school. My younger sister was still a baby. 'Come, I'll take you to her,' she said, holding my hand and leading the way. I met Rekha for the first time. She was pretty, and her eyes were lined with mascara. She said her name was Bhanurekha. 'What is your father's name?' I asked. 'Gemini Ganesan,' came the pat reply. My eyes filled with tears. How can that be? He was my father.

When Chinamma came to take me home, I blurted out the story. 'Never mind,' she said. Another day I pointed Rekha out to Chinamma, and she said, 'She is like your sister. And she's pretty.' Then, there was Rekha's younger sister, Radha, who was even prettier, I thought. Her resemblance to Appa was startling. When I was a little older, I learnt that they were born to Pushpavalli and Appa, and that they lived with their mother and had other siblings too.

Appa's relationship with Pushpavalli was perhaps his first outside his marriage, and from the way they remained friends till the end, exchanging pleasantries and enquiring after each other's families, they seemed comfortable with their past. There was no trace of bitterness. And from Rekha and Radha's accounts, their mother had nothing but good things to say, not only about Appa, but also Bobjima. 'Though he has never lived with us, we 'felt' his presence wherever we went or whatever we did as my mother was constantly talking about him. She told us of his likes and dislikes. Whatever you wish to call it – love, attraction, affection – the feeling my mother had towards him was definitely a strong and positive one that lasted throughout her life. She

FACING PAGE:

Gemini-Savithri

Fans of both actors would call out their names in a hyphenated form – 'Gemini-Savithri'. Theirs was an endearing chemistry, both on and off the screen.

Trailblazer

Pushpavalli, the beautiful Telugu actress, and Appa had a brief romantic relationship, which was perhaps his first outside his marriage, but they remained friends till the end. They had two children – Rekha and Radha.

gave us whatever memories we have of a father; memories we treasure and cherish,' says Rekha.

Radha, who lives in the U.S. with her husband, Usman Syed, and sons, Naveed and Aman, has, in a manner of speaking, made up for at least some of that lost time with Appa. Each time Appa went to the U.S. to be with Revathi, he would visit Radha too on the west coast, and spend some days with her and her family. She says, 'I have some very pleasant and poignant memories of the father I came to know and I shall always treasure them. I appreciate and cherish the fact that Appa was with us on my son Naveed's high school graduation day, taking part in the festivities and blessing him.' Rekha was born on 10 October 1954, and Radha on 17 November (Appa's birthday) the following year.

Pushpavalli, it seems, was unaware that Appa was a married man when she fell for him, and much against his conscience that kept pricking him, Appa began to reciprocate. She was a beautiful and accomplished woman; it would have been hard indeed to spurn her love. It is not as though Appa was a passive recipient of flattering attention from women. He was good looking, charming, and he enjoyed being adored and wooed. He loved his first family, but that did not stand in the way of his submitting to temptation. His relationships were certainly not one-sided. This fact must have preyed on his mind in later years; of the hurt he caused Bobjima and his mother and aunt, and much later, his children. And also the hurt and pain that his lady-loves must have gone through when their fairytale romance ended.

Pushpavalli passed away in 1991 of complications related to diabetes. To me, she was Pushpavalli Aunty, who would give me huge jars of mango and lemon pickles she prepared herself. She was soft-spoken and affectionate, and had only good things to say about Bobjima and Gangamma. Her children, too, have taken after her.

Rekha and Radha respected Bobjima a great deal. It was, they said, dinned into their heads by their mother that she was an extraordinary person, a *devata* (goddess-like). Rekha says she has 'inherited' some of Bobjima's qualities! Once when Rekha came visiting, sometime before Appa fell seriously ill, Bobjima insisted on buying her a new cellphone. Rekha was touched. Amma was very interested in electronics. She would seek out the latest models and contraptions. She was good at fixing electrical appliances, too. Appa couldn't even operate the television without her help.

Unlike Pushpavalli, Savithri walked into a relationship with Appa with her eyes wide open, though she was a slip of a girl, barely into

Photo album

Seated left to right: Appa, Bobjima with a dressed up Radha on the day of her baby shower, when she was expecting her first child. Her mother Pushpavalli is standing behind them. On the right is a photograph of Rekha during her early years in Bollywood. It was found in Appa's personal collection of photographs.

her sixteenth year. She knew he was a married man with children. She probably did not know then of his relationship with Pushpavalli. Theirs was a sustained union that lasted for more than a dozen years, with a marriage, household and children. The Gemini-Savithri real and reel life combination did wonders for them in their private as well as screen life.

When Appa contracted typhoid, Chinamma took us children to see him. There was this beautiful woman in white attending to him. I exclaimed to Chinamma, 'What a beautiful nurse!' Ouch. Chinamma had pinched my thigh. She motioned me to be quiet. Once we were out of the 'hospital', I burst out, 'Why did you pinch me?' Chinamma pacified me and said something by way of explanation. Years later, when I remembered the incident and recounted it to her, she laughed. 'That wasn't a hospital, that was Savithri's home.' And the beautiful nurse was Savithri.

Some years after that, I would spend many Sundays and other holidays playing with Viji in Savithri Aunty's house on Habibullah Road. Strangely, no one at home forbade me from going there. The house was so much like our own, even the mosaic patterns on the floor were similar. Initially, I had no idea who they were, and that didn't bother me. I was busy having a good time. There would be lots of goodies to eat, games to play, and in their backyard, they kept pets that included lovebirds. Once Savithri Aunty brought a couple of leopard cubs from Kodaikanal but had to return them to the forest department after Appa convinced her that it was not a good idea to keep wild creatures confined at home.

When Viji and I would tire of playing games, her grandmother

P.S:- I'm sending a letter that was sent for you I misplaced it & that's why I could send it to you earlier.

5/14/95

My dearest daddy,

It's only been two weeks since you left but I feel its donkey's years already. That's because you bring so much light & life wherever you go ~~that~~ they feel the void as soon as you leave.

Usman, Naveed & Aman often talk about how well you look and about your spontaneous sense of humour. All my friends like Monica (photoshop), Lalitha, (the jewelry shop lady), Leelaji (the lady who took us to the Livermore temple) remember you a lot and talk about you very fondly.

I called Revathi Akka yesterday as I knew she must be missing you after your long visit with her. It was really nice having a nice warm chat with her. She told me about the fun trip to Europe with Kamala Akka. I wanted Akka to give me Narayani's address but she said as she moved she didn't have her new address. Please write to me her address as I would like to write to her as she could use some mental support from people who love her.

Nothing has happened about your interview in India post yet. As soon as it is published I'll send you a copy.

Happy together

Above: Radha, Gangamma and Appa with Radha's husband Usman standing behind them.
Below: Rekha and Radha, beautiful sisters who look a lot like each other.

Letter from a daughter

Radha's letter to Appa written after he returned to India, following his visit to her home in the U.S. She is a happy person, loving and giving as is evident from what she writes .

I hope you received the pictures I sent you. I'm sorry I didn't find time to even write a note to you at that time. I also mailed quite a few pictures of you to Rekha the same time. I'm sure she'll call me after receiving its. I'll let me know when I next time talk with her.

Mother's day is this Sunday. Viswan pampers me as always & this time for Mother's day he is treating me at the Hyatt Regency for a body message with essential aromatic oils & pedicure to sooth my tired feet as he says. I sometimes wonder what I did to deserve such a special humanbeing as my life partner.

At this time of the year I have poignant memories of Amma & feel nostalgic about the times I spent with her & you during her last days. when we went shopping for fresh fish & so on. The day of her passing away went by this year with out just tears. I prayed for her peace & your long healthy & happy life.

How are you Appa? I'm glad you stay busy. Revathi Akka told me that you & Bobji are in Delhi right now. I'm sure you both will give Narayani & her kids some strength.

Convey my love to Kamala Akka, Giji, her children, daughter & all at home. I hope Bobji Amma liked the color of her saree.

Miss you a lot. We love you tremendously. Swamy & the kids send their love to you all.

Take care & keep smiling. Your ever loving child
Sasha

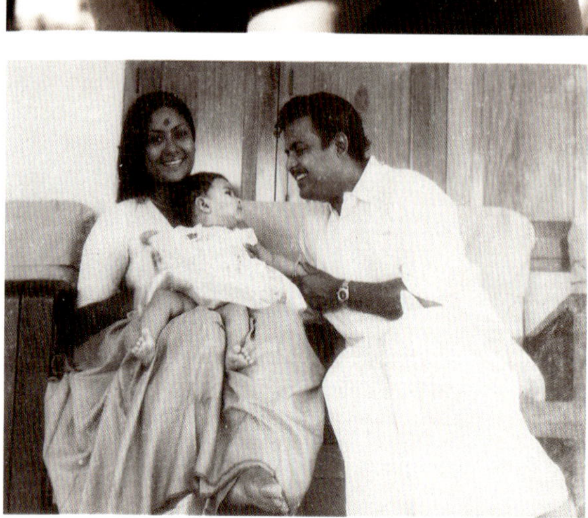

(Savithri Aunty's mother, Subhadramma) would sit us down and talk to us or feed us. There would be many visitors and relatives in and out of the house, and sometimes, large baskets of fragrant mangoes would arrive from Andhra. Once I met a relative who was visiting from their village in Andhra. She looked really old. She was half-reclining on a cot and was smoking a desi cigar (rolled tobacco). So cool, I thought. It was exciting to be there!

Vijayachamundeshwari, Viji for short, was born to Appa and Savithri on 2 December 1958. They had married secretly at the Chamundi temple at Mysore during the making of their first film together, *Manam Pola Mangalyam* ('A Marriage of Minds') sometime in end-1952. But they disclosed their marriage only in 1956 when they started living together. They named their first child after the deity that had presided over their wedding. Seven years later, on 18 August 1965, came Sathish. The children had English-speaking nannies to take care of them.

When I was in the sixth standard, Viji told me she was going to Bombay with her mother. Savithri Aunty had to shoot for a Hindi film, *Ganga Ki Leheren* ('Waves of the Ganga'). I wanted to go too. I begged and pleaded with Appa till he gave in. I went, and spent wonderful days at the Airlines Hotel in Bombay, going to the studios, watching some shooting, eating lots, and listening to stories. Towards the end of the trip, Viji and I were taken along to a party. When introducing us, Aunty would say, 'These are my children, number one and number two,' pointing first to me and then to Viji.

Before going to bed at night, Aunty would lie between Viji and I and tell us stories. I so wanted a fringe and nagged Aunty for a haircut. She said it was not possible, for she feared that we would earn the displeasure of the grandmothers and Bobjima back home. I promised to take all the blame and finally, she took me to a Chinese saloon and I came out beaming, with a fringe.

On returning to Madras, as I entered the house, Chinamma shrieked, 'Look, she's gone and cut her hair. We should never have sent her.' I gallantly defended SavithriAunty, saying it was done at my insistence. Of course, that was the truth. Peace prevailed once they learnt I was taken good care of, that I had been fed well, and so on. Chinamma lapped up all

TOP:

We are family

Appa, Sathish and Viji in a happy mood. Baby Sathish always had a big black bindi *drawn on his forehead 'to ward off evil spirits', his maternal grandmother told me when I asked why a boy should wear a* bindi.

FACING PAGE:

Second household

Top left: Appa holding Vijayachamundeswari in his arms, his first child with Savithri. Top right: Savithri Aunty loved animals and here she is holding a leopard cub on a leash. After a few days, she returned the cub to the wild in Kodaikanal. Below: Savithri Aunty and Appa with baby Sathish, their second child.

TOP:

Daddy dearest

Viji giving Appa a tight hug when he was past eighty in Chennai.

RIGHT:

An affectionate letter

Appa wrote this letter to Viji when she and I were studying at the Presentation Convent boarding school in Kodaikanal in 1966-67. It's an affectionate letter to a child who was barely eight, and perhaps was missing her family. The letter is written on the letterhead of a production company that Savithri Aunty had started, naming it after her daughter: Vijaya Chamundeswari Pictures. Curiously, the only production company that Appa started was named after me: Sri Narayani Films!

VIJAYA *Chamundeswari* PICTURES

MOTION PICTURE PRODUCERS & DISTRIBUTORS

Madras Branch :
11, HABIBULLAH ROAD, T'NAGAR
MADRAS-17
Phone : 87293

Head Office :
74, 3rd. MAIN RD. SANTHINAGAR COLONY
HYDERABAD-28 (A.P.)
Phone :

22/2/67

Our darling child Viji,

We are in receipt of your nice letter and we are happy to know you and Naraya are getting on well. You said they have cut your hair and We think you must be looking very nice with the 'bob' hair do. Do you like the food? Narayani has written that she likes the food. How is your cough now? Do not expose your throat and chest to the chilly air. You two must behave very well and get a name as the two best children at the school.

I wrote to Rev. Mother John requesting her to put Narayani in ~~class V~~ i.e. Form V. I do not know what happened. Take care of your health. Ask Narayani to write about what happened to her going to Form V?

Study well, play well and eat well. If you want anything tell Mother.

Here your little brother and all are O.K. Everyone is happy after seeing your letter and nobody cries now!

Keep all these letters carefully and do not throw them away. We are keeping your letters.

With all love & blessings
Your dear dear baba
& mummy
Santi Ganesh

See who's here

Appa, Rekha and Revathi at Revathi's house in Chennai, with Rekha holding a wedding photograph of my parents, Appa and Bobjima. She had come to visit an ailing Bobjima at G.G. Hospital.

the details as she usually did after my visits to Aunty's house.

Appa wished for me to go to a boarding school – Presentation Convent in Kodaikanal. I was studying in a branch of the same school in Madras. Much to my excitement, he sought admission for me there and got it. Meanwhile, Savithri Aunty decided to send Viji there as well, since we were good friends and I would be her older sister and take care of her. I was in the ninth standard and Viji in the fourth, and we loved it there.

Bobjima came to visit me at the school, and found me with oil-less hair and in a short skirt riding high above my knees. I had attained puberty a few months earlier. Bobjima did not approve of the situation and pulled me out of the school. Back in Chennai, I was admitted to the Banaras Matriculation School at the Andhra Mahila Sabha, Mylapore, because I refused to go back to my old school. In Kodai, I had opted out of mathematics and taken up typing and shorthand instead. The only other place where you could avoid mathematics was if you did a Banaras Matric. Without me, Viji too was back in Madras at the insistence of her grandmother, and she was admitted to Vidyodaya School. We were growing up and saw each other less frequently or not at all after that.

Our interaction with Sathish really began only after Savithri Aunty passed away after a long diabetic coma. At the time he was still in high school, and came to live with us.

'When I first came to live with Appa and Bobjima, I was confused about many things. I was traumatized by the sudden changes in my life. I didn't have an open mind about him (Appa). I had a lot of preconceived notions. But those two years I lived in that house helped me exorcise all the ghosts of the past,' says Sathish. He poured out his feelings and fears in a diary that Appa chanced to read. When Sathish confronted him about this, insisting that what he did was wrong – to have read his diary without his permission – Appa replied that he was more concerned about dispelling Sathish's fears.

A frank exchange followed in which Appa conceded that it was indeed not right for him to have read his diary, but they agreed that a channel of communication had opened up and from then on, barriers were broken

All decked up

At Deepu's wedding reception (1999). Left to right: Viji, Narayani, Sathish, Gigi, Revathi and Kamala. Identical saris, Kamala continues with Appa's tradition!

and they became friends. 'If only he'd been less entangled in emotional involvements and focused more on his work, things might have been very different,' muses Sathish, who says those two years contributed a great deal to shape his personality and outlook, for the better.

I can't say what really went though Bobjima's mind at this time; but she did her best to make Sathish feel at home. In a way, she remained detached, carrying on with her normal routine and interests. Gigi was the only sibling left in the house by the time Sathish came to live there, and none of us resented his presence because we knew he'd been through very rough times.

He was given a room on the top floor, where he hung a large oil portrait of his mother. Our hearts ached for him, but by then we were busy with our own lives in different places. Sathish had been through a lot; he had ministered to a mother who was bedridden and unconscious; she who was once so beautiful and spontaneous, an actress par excellence much loved by thousands of fans. During those years, he and Appa had the opportunity to spend time together, to try and understand one another, and share their thoughts and feelings.

Sathish says he learnt a lot from Bobjima, especially with regard to personal and kitchen hygiene, and the importance of not wasting food. Every day, she would give him a glass of milk with Horlicks. He didn't much care for it and would quietly tip it over the balcony. When he was discovered many weeks later, she sat him down and gave him a piece of her mind and impressed upon him that it was criminal to waste food.

Sathish went on to study engineering in Bangalore and married his schoolmate, Prasanna. They live in the U.S. and have a son, Pradyumna. Sathish is probably the bravest of all of Appa's children. His childhood was traumatic; his parents had separated, and his mother, though she continued acting in films, grew progressively vulnerable and weak. She would fall ill and Sathish would have to keep an eye on her, though he was barely into his teens, as she took to alcohol. Yet he is among the finest, with a sensitive mind and calm disposition. He loves music and cricket, and has a keen interest in philosophy.

Appa and Savithri fell out some time in 1969-70. Was it because his name was being linked with another actress? Were the pressures of two households causing fissures in their relationship? Or were there differences in the way they looked at their future, both in terms of career and family responsibilities? One cannot say with certainty. Maybe it was a combination of all these factors. Since they are not here to clarify things, and I have not heard details firsthand, I can only say that the break-up left a terrible aftermath in both their lives. They were never the same again. After their separation, Savithri produced a film that did badly. She went through difficulties in her personal life, lost a lot of money, had tax problems, and her health took a turn for the worse. She became alcohol-dependent and her diabetic condition worsened, leaving her in a coma from which she never woke up.

All boys' club

Appa with his grandsons Aman and Naveed (Radha and Usman's children) in the U.S.

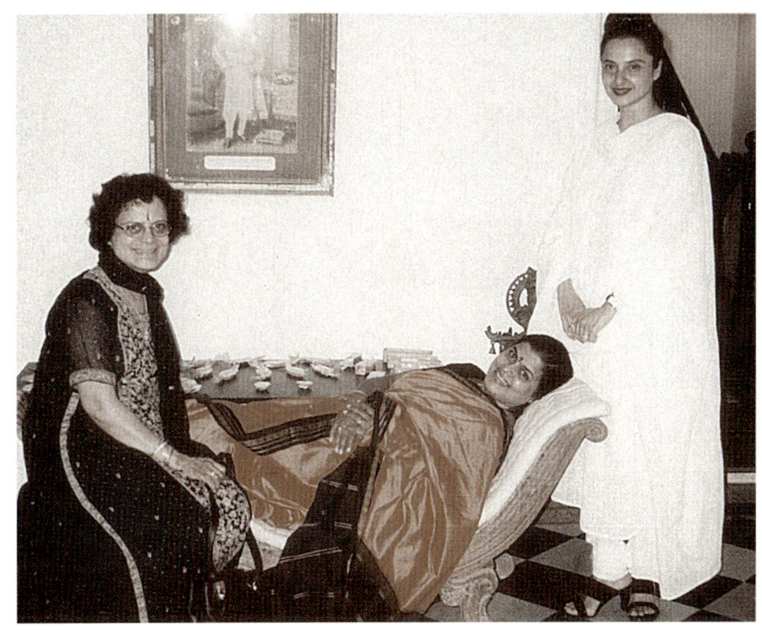

LEFT:

Shop till you drop

At Amethyst, an upscale boutique in Gopalapuram, Chennai, a favourite haunt of Rekha's. Revathi and Rekha look on amused as I collapse on a couch there.

RIGHT:

Giddy buddies

Radha, Kamala and Viji giggling, striking poses and perhaps doing a mimic act.

And Appa? He did get involved with other women, though not in the way he had with either Pushpavalli or Savithri, who were women of substance who were fiercely independent, with strong personalities. While Pushpavalli remained friends with him till her last days, Savithri didn't have an option as destiny took over her health and life.

From all accounts, Appa loved Pushpavalli and Savithri. As for his other, fleeting, extra-marital relationships, let's say they were neither serious nor spontaneous. He seemed to be seeking refuge from reality; he craved adoration and appreciation. Bobjima learnt to survive all the heartaches and misunderstandings through sheer patience. She remained a dignified and devoted woman, with strong family responsibilities and commitments, with an avid interest in a range of activities she had cultivated over the years while her husband had been busy both in his professional and private life. She read a lot, listened to music, attended to her children and in-laws' needs, reared cows, had many pets, and traveled to pilgrimage destinations like Badrinath and Kedarnath.

Bobjima loved Appa deeply; she was utterly devoted to him. But she just could not bring herself to be what he would have liked her to be now – an adoring, social companion who encouraged and praised his every action, after all those years of having to share him with another. They were now at a stage when their needs were quite different – she, a detached but loving wife and mother, he, a distraught, repentant and vulnerable man who sorely needed to be fussed over and comforted, never mind if it meant making more mistakes.

CHAPTER SIX
Beyond Cinema

Where the clear stream of reason has not lost its way
Into the dreary desert sand of dead habit.

– Rabindranath Tagore

Appa being an avid sportsman and follower of cricket, tennis, billiards, golf and what have you, would often take us children to the stadium in Chennai to witness these matches, from the prized pavilion seats. It is surprising, then, that none of us took to active sports. Revathi and Kamala played a lot of table-tennis in school and college, winning matches. Revathi played throwball in school and Kamala, netball.

I have never been a sportsperson. Nor have I much interest in spectator sports except for some five-day cricket test matches that interested me more for their celebrity and entertainment value than the game itself. Gigi and her husband play table-tennis and watch matches on television when time permits. Sathish did play a lot of cricket in school, and would come home black as soot, tanned to the bone. He wrote to his siblings the following email, after Appa passed away in 2005, and I reproduce here an abridged version:

FACING PAGE:

Game, set, match!

Appa flanked by tennis mates at the Mambalam Tennis Club, Chennai, where he would play a couple of vigorous games of tennis every morning, and return home with telltale sambar *stains on his white t-shirt, having feasted on steaming* idlis *and* vadas *at a café!*

RIGHT:

Making sports news

A newspaper clipping from The Hindu *dated 16 October 1972, that I found pasted on a page of his Hoe & Co. diary of the same date. Besides being a good cricket and tennis player, Appa was a billiards champ as well.*

BILLIARDS

R. Ganesh Beats Ethiraj

MADRAS, Oct. 16.

When film star 'Gemini,' R. Ganesh came to inaugurate the second Madras United Club open billiards and snooker tournament, at MUC last evening, he was not merely performing a formal function. He played a snooker match against T. V. Ethiraj, the member-in-charge, won it and moved up in the tournament.

It was a pleasant surprise to the audience that Ganesh could play the game so well. His potting was fine and he won 54-31, 24-66, 58-21, 44-36.

In the billiards match that followed R. Rajagopal beat Ashok Hinduja 615-472. Initially it looked as if Rajagopal would have smooth sailing. But in the last half hour of the two-hour session, Hinduja came within 40 points of his opponent. But Rajagopal with good finishing spell clinched the issue.

The tournament, which will be a curtain-raiser to the National to be held here in December has attracted several prominent entries, including A. Savoor of Bangalore, knocking at the doors of International honours, the flashy Omar Rehman also from Bangalore, S. A. Aleem, the State billiards champion and V. B. Khanderia, the State snooker champion.

It was in 1976 that I got to see a live cricket test match – the venue was Chepauk Stadium, Chennai – for the very first time in my life. The two teams were India and the West Indies. Mummy told me that I was going to see my first live test cricket match and that too with Daddy (I used to call him Daddy, then). I was as excited as any eleven-year-old Indian boy would be, going to witness a live cricket test match and that too, for the first time.

The driver dropped me off at Daddy's house. I had packed a bag with water, jam sandwiches and a hand towel.

Daddy and I drove to Chepauk Stadium. He parked the car and we made our way to the pavilion. Uncle Nagesh, the comedy actor, greeted us on the way. He asked me, 'Are you a batsman or bowler?' I replied, 'I'm an all-rounder.' 'Okay,' he said. 'Show me a forward defence stroke.' As I attempted to do that, he came forward and corrected my final position – the bat held close to the stretched out left leg without a gap for the ball to go through. Daddy informed me later that Uncle Nagesh was a good sportsman and a great cricket fan.

We made our way to our seats. Daddy pulled out a large pair of binoculars. That was the first time I looked through a pair of binoculars. He helped me hold it steady as it was very heavy for me and I finally got to take a closer look at the faces of the great Clive Lloyd, Andy Roberts, Vanburn Holder and Lance Gibbs.

I was a huge fan of the West Indies team then. Mummy was a very big fan of Garfield Sobers. Maybe because he was a lefty, like Mom was. I wonder who was Daddy's favourite. Funny, I never got to ask him that. Back then my cricket mates and I would take pride in being able to remember long names: Isaac Vivian Alexander Richards, Alvin Isaac Kallicharran, Lancelot Richard Gibbs and Anderson Montgomery Everton Roberts.

As I watched through those huge binoculars at Clive Lloyd giving the ball a mighty whack, and as the ball soared skywards, my heart was in my mouth as the ball reached dizzying heights and finally made its way down to be gobbled up by one of the many giant hands of the Windies chaps. I told Daddy that these guys are going to massacre us puny Indians, to which he said, 'Just wait and watch.'

We watched the game all the five days. I saw Gundappa Vishwanath carve his elegant and stylish square cuts to every thundering and blistering ball sent down by Roberts and team. I saw my Dad's face beaming with pride at every stroke. He explained how every stroke was played or how it should have been played. I still remember the noise and din the crowd made for every shot from Vishy's blade. I remember my father carrying me on his shoulders and jumping with joy when India won the test match.

Every day I would go back home and re-live the entire day to Mummy, who would listen patiently. I wondered why she had a tear in her eye then. Now I know. Thanks, Pa.

Two years later, I actually got to see Daddy play in a live cricket match. I also had the rare opportunity to play with Daddy. It was the 1979 star cricket match in Coimbatore. Daddy picked me up from school and we were off to Coimbatore for the match. I cannot forget the soaring sixes he hit in his sixty-four runs not out. They couldn't get him out. I was the non-striker. This time it was I who was beaming with pride. When it was our turn to bowl, I took seven wickets. I still remember V.S. Raghavan, the actor, refusing to leave the pitch for an L.B.W. on my bowling and being run out at the very next ball.

All this just seems like yesterday. Every moment is etched in my memory. Maybe because Daddy made that happen.

By the way, I still have those binoculars safely tucked away in a locker. Maybe I should bring them out for a cricket match with my eleven-year-old son.

Love,
Sathish

LEFT:

Cricket with Appa

An email sent by Sathish about his experience of going to a test cricket match with Appa for the first time. A cricket enthusiast, Sathish would come home tanned to the bone while in high school, having played cricket in the scorching midday sun.

BOTTOM:

Place in the sun

Right to left: Viji, Sathish, Appa and Prasanna posing outside Viji's home on Habibullah Road in Chennai. In place of the house today stands an office complex, with a terraced flat on the topmost floor where Viji lives with her family.

In later years, Appa and Bobjima installed two television sets in their bedroom. Appa would watch tennis, golf or cricket matches with the volume turned up. Seated beside him on the bed, Bobjima would watch her serials, volume muted. 'How on earth can you know what they're saying, Amma?' I would ask her and she would scowl, pointing to Appa, 'He doesn't let me sit in the hall where I can watch television; he wants me to sit with him.' Strange, I thought. Their kinship was funny, even touching.

Appa's other passion was food – cooking as well as feeding others. I've learnt more from Appa about cooking than I have from Bobjima, Chinamma or Gangamma. They were more interested in making stuff and feeding us than imparting lessons. They would shoo us children out of the kitchen during cooking hours. But Appa was different. If you showed some interest, or appreciated what he had cooked, he would set about explaining how he did it and throw in a bit about how one could improvise with the recipe.

Shutting his eyes and shrugging his shoulders in an expression of half-disgust, half-dismissal, I remember Appa once describing the taste of coffee our newly-appointed cook had concocted. 'This coffee tastes like milk extracted from the pith of a banana tree – it's absolutely tasteless and odourless.' What followed was a lesson on how to make delicious coffee. 'Never boil the decoction. Heat the milk first, take it off the stove and then add the required amount of freshly brewed decoction. Boiling coffee kills taste,' he explained. I was in my teens, and darted sympathetic looks at the nervous cook who looked ready to burst into tears. Cook Mani, however, went on to become an expert coffee maker, thanks to the Gemini lesson.

Appa's trademark instant tiffin item was *uppuma*, made with large-grain *rava* (semolina) and generous portions of ghee, mustard seeds, fresh ginger, onions, lemon juice, and curry leaves. He would wield the *sattuvam* (perforated flat ladle) with grace, turning the *uppuma* over gently at frequent intervals so that it did not stick to the *illupachatti* (wok). He was a terrific cook, as his mother was, and would experiment often, but well within the limits offered by traditional hand-me-down recipes.

I learnt how to make *pahakkai pitlay* from Appa. The bitter gourd preparation is made with lentil, spices, coconut and tamarind. 'Don't peel off the skin and don't remove the seeds,' he would say. 'You'll kill it if you do.' During a ten-day break he took to be with me in Delhi, I would enter the kitchen only to hand him ingredients and clean up the mess afterwards. Pottering in the kitchen was like oxygen for him. He loved to cook and would want to do everything himself – from buying the vegetable and washing it, to cutting and cooking it. He would insist on serving large portions to everyone, and later I would go house to house in

Old friends meet

Outside her home in Delhi: Vyjayantimala with Appa and I. He presented her with a bouquet of red roses on the occasion.

the neighbourhood, distributing food, as Appa did not believe in making small quantities. I would get irritated at times, and would suggest we go out for a meal. 'Why? You don't like what I make?' he would ask dejectedly, and that would settle the issue.

Sathish has taken after Appa in this respect, and though his job as a software engineer in California leaves him with little time for anything else, he cooks whenever he can. When I lamented that I never sat down with Appa, in his later years when he had the time, and wrote down all his wonderful recipes, Sathish promptly emailed me one of Appa's favourites, Garlic *vathakuzhambu* – peeled whole pods of garlic cooked in a gravy of tamarind extract, black pepper paste and spices.

For this dish, Appa would peel the garlic himself, grind the pepper and other spices on the *ammi*, the grinding stone, extract tamarind juice, carefully sieving the liquid to remove any trace of sand or seed, and watch over the fire as the concoction bubbled away. Phone calls and visitors would have to be taken to the kitchen for he would not budge from his vantage position till he'd finished with the ritual.

TOP:

Read and relax

In his first home in Chennai, seated on his favourite chair, leafing through a regional language magazine.

LEFT:

His first motorcar

Appa with his first motorcar, a Ford. Its original colour was light green, but he later chose to paint it a deep blue, his favourite colour. The Ford is now part of Kamala's husband Selvaraj's collection of vintage vehicles.

EAST LYNNE

This novel was made into a tamil film 'Thai Ullam' 'தாய் உள்ளம்' by Messrs. Narayanan Co. Madras in 1952. in which I played the villain Sir Francis Levison. M.V. Rajamma played the heroine and R.S. Manohar played the hero directed by K. Ramnoth. A famous song was sung by M.L. Vasantha Kumari '[illegible]' which became very popular.

G.G. Appa

East Lynne

An excited Appa wrote this on the first page of East Lynne, *when he spotted the tattered book in my bookshelf at my home in Delhi. It was in fact Bobjima who gave the book to me to read, perhaps when I was in college, but I was unaware that Appa had essayed one of the characters in the novel.*

Hungry, Appa once said he'd like to eat Maggie noodles. Okay, I said, and immersed the instant noodles and masala in boiling water as per instructions on the packet. 'Two minutes,' I said. 'Let's go and sit in the living room. It's cooler there.' He stood there, watching intently as the noodles were getting cooked. He wanted to make sure. Once done, I transferred the noodles into a bowl. Impatient, he couldn't wait and burnt his tongue. Like a child, I thought. I never could ask him the questions that often surfaced in my mind. Why did he have all those extra-marital relationships? Why did he have to have children outside his marriage? Why did he get bored so easily? How come he was so attached to all of us? Did he feel guilty about not being faithful to Bobjima?

'Here, you have some,' he said, pushing the bowl in my direction and the reverie was broken. I smiled. Affectionate and demonstrative, Appa could charm his way out of any situation.

In Delhi in 1994 to perform as *sutradhar* (anchor) in an English language play staged by a German theatre group, Appa was to stay at Hotel Ashok, a good hour's drive from where I lived in north Delhi. Every day, I would take him to an Udupi restaurant for breakfast. One day we were eating dosas with a friend. 'See,' he said to her, holding the fork like you would a pitchfork and glancing at a gentleman at the table next to us. 'Some people eat as though they are digging a grave.' We giggled and laughed through the meal, as he regaled us with funny stories. He also made jokes about how etiquette demands that you spoon the soup away from you 'as though you are feeding the person seated opposite you'.

My parents loved my modest little flat tucked away in 'remote' north Delhi, with its small rooms and tiny kitchen. They looked forward to coming here, even if for a few days, and while my mother busied herself reading or watching television, or walking and chatting with neighbours and friends, my father would declare, 'I'm B-O-R-E-D. Don't go to work today. Let's go out somewhere.' Bobjima would be happy to stay home with Muffin, the golden retriever, and I would set off with Appa, visiting friends, most of whom were in south Delhi.

'I wish to visit Vyjayanti,' he declared one day. He meant Vyjayantimala, the actress, who had moved to Hindi cinema following a fairly successful stint in Tamil filmdom. The drive to Vyjayanti's home was a disaster, as my car's ageing 800 cc engine got overheated – I'd got an air-conditioner installed just before Appa's arrival in Delhi that summer. But the thirty-kilometer ride stressed the engine and by the time we reached Lodhi Estate, our destination, the car was spewing smoke. We had to ask for buckets of water to cool the radiator and just as we were finishing up the damage control, Vy appeared, arms laden with shopping bags, looking as beautiful as ever, the smoke from the car framing her as she approached us smiling broadly.

It was flashback time, and I listened with interest as the two exchanged stories and tidbits over cups of freshly brewed south Indian coffee and snacks served in bright melaware plates. When I remarked that the *bajjis* (fritters) were delicious, Vy was quick to say, 'If your father says so, then I'd be convinced!' Everyone in the film industry and Gemini's friends and acquaintances were familiar with his penchant for cooking (and eating). I seem to have taken after him but only as far as far as a love of food is concerned. My cooking wouldn't measure up to his standards.

Everything wasn't all that perfect with Appa's cooking, though. When he was in a rush, he would dunk *paalak* (spinach) and other greens without washing them properly, and we would end up munching sand uncomplainingly. Bobjima, dripping sarcasm, would mutter under her breath, 'I wouldn't feed this even to the cows.' Appa made yummy *rasam*, full of spices, garnished with generous dollops of clarified butter and fresh coriander. If you drank it hot and in copious quantities, it doubled as an effective system-cleanser and banished colds and coughs.

Bargaining with vegetable vendors was one of Appa's favourite indulgences first thing in the morning. Kamala would linger behind him, busy paying off the balance money that he'd bargained so hard for, as he went blissfully ahead, arguing and choosing aubergines ('the skin should be tight, look out for wormholes'), drumsticks ('fatter the better') and okra ('if the tip breaks off with a snap, it's fresh'). Kamala would argue with Appa, 'Why do you bargain with these poor vegetable sellers? Why don't you just give them what they ask for?' And Appa would sit there, eyes downcast, like an errant schoolboy.

FACING PAGE:

Pilgrim Trail

Above: Appa and Bobjima in a boat on the Ganga in Varanasi, where they went to celebrate his sixtieth birthday. Bobjima told me several years later that Appa went off to see a movie with some friends he met there one evening, when she refused to go with him!

Below: An exhausted Bobjima and Appa standing before the Amarnath ice lingam *shrine in Jammu and Kashmir, when we visited the state in the 1980s.*

Appa was a keen sportsman but his passion was cooking. Lucky you if he decided it was time to give you a break from the kitchen. His creations were absolutely divine. Woe to you, though, if you had no help, for you would have to clean up after the master chef while he got absorbed in a tennis match on television! Here's the recipe for a Gemini Special.

Milagu Kuzhambu

(Black Peppercorn Curry)

Ingredients

Whole black peppercorns ....**2 tbsp**

Yellow lentil *(Arhar in Hindi, Thuvaram paruppu in Tamil)*............**1 tbsp**

Yellow lentil *(Chana dal in Hindi, Kadalai paruppu in Tamil)*..........**1 tbsp**

White lentil *(White urad dal in Hindi, Ulutham paruppu in Tamil)*...**1 tbsp**

Rice...**1 tsp**

Fresh curry leaves..**A handful**

Whole *dhania* seeds..**1 tsp**

Asafoetida...**A large pinch**

Whole red chillies...**Three**

Mustard seeds..**1 tsp**

Peeled garlic fried in ghee................................**100-250 g** (*optional*)

Gingelly oil *(til oil in Hindi, nallennai in Tamil)*.......................**1 tbsp**

Tamarind ball the size of two lemons, soaked for 30 minutes

Jaggery...**one inch piece** (*optional*)

Salt to taste

Method

Fry all lentils, rice, *dhania* seeds, peppercorns and red chillies in gingelly oil. Once they turn golden, add curry leaves and toss well. Keep aside. Heat the remaining gingelly oil in a deep pan and fry mustard seeds until they splutter. Lower the flame and add asafoetida. Add the squeezed tamarind juice and boil it with salt.

Meanwhile, wet-grind the fried lentil mix on a stone or electric grinder. Once the tamarind water is cooked, lower the flame and blend the ground lentil mixture in and add the piece of jaggery. After a while also add the ghee-roasted garlic. Once the liquid has thickened, remove the vessel from the stove. Garnish with fresh curry leaves.

Serve

Serve with steaming hot rice and ghee to taste. It could be eaten with roast *pappad* (*appalam* in Tamil) and roasted potato (*urulai* roast in Tamil) and *paruppu thogayal* (roasted *arhar dal* ground with red chillies, asafoetida and salt).

Food, glorious food

Kamala and I stuffing our faces with aloo parathas *at a rundown canteen in Shimla, barely a few minutes after a sumptuous breakfast at an upscale hotel, much to the horror of a friend who was poised with the camera. 'I'll record your gluttony for posterity,' she declared.*

The vendors loved him. They came to say goodbye to him as he lay in state, howling, 'Who will now bargain with us like you did? Who will linger on, chatting and enquiring after us?'

Appa was equally enterprising when it came to sniffing out south Indian hotels and restaurants in the unlikeliest of places. In the early 1990s, Appa, Bobjima and I had set off on an unusual pilgrimage to Hardwar and Rishikesh. Truthfully, it was a way we'd figured of rejuvenating Appa's spirits after a particularly harrowing time he'd had, a kind of post-midlife crisis. He wasn't feeling too well, and he'd come to Delhi as chairman of the jury for the National Film Awards – an assignment he chose to withdraw from due to inclement health. Okay, I said, now that you're here, we might as well make the most of it instead of moping at home. Where do you want to go? I asked. He promptly said, 'Hardwar-Rishikesh.' And that's where we went.

We spent an evening at the Dayananda Saraswati Ashram in Rishikesh, with its own access to the Ganga, the very picture of tranquility. On that particular day, the ashram had several visitors including many from outside India. They were filing into a newly-built hall, where the stage was set for a talk. We followed the queue. 'Who is going to talk?' I asked. 'Swami Dayananda Saraswati is here; he will address the gathering himself,' I was told. My mother, father and I sat somewhere in the rear, as the seats were fast filling up.

At the appointed time, the Swami came on stage and announced, 'We have a special guest amidst us today. I request Mr Ganesan, the popular movie actor from south India, to come and address the gathering.' I nudged Appa. 'He's talking about you, Pa.' My heart was pounding. Would Appa talk sense? What would he say? Appa got up, smiled shyly, and walked towards the mike. He looked at the audience, straight, and said, 'I am totally unprepared for this. I came here as a visitor like anyone else, and was waiting to hear Swamiji speak. However, now that he expects me to talk, I couldn't possible let him down...' Amma and I exchanged worried glances. What would he say? He wasn't even prepared for this sort of thing. And he was just trying to come out of a self-inflicted bout of deep sadness. What if he said things that didn't make any sense? Oh dear, dear, dear...

Clear as a bell, Appa's steady voice rang through the makeshift auditorium. 'Unprepared as I am to deliver a talk at this august ashram, it would be appropriate for me to talk about nothing.' My heart fluttered but went back to its regular beat when he completed the sentence, '... nothing as in everything, or zero. Infinity, if you like. What fills the space from zero to infinity? Nothing, and everything.' His talk was a perfect spiel of everything and nothing, aptly cosmic, free of mundane specifics. He talked of science and spirituality, of Vedanta and Vigyan, Einstein and Ashtavakra, Tennyson and Thiruvalluvar, ascetics and actors. I looked at Amma who was beaming with pride. When Appa returned to his seat, I hugged him in relief as he asked, 'Was I okay?' That was an unforgettable and enlightening experience. 'Never underestimate him,' I said to Amma.

'I want *jeera rasam*, black pepper *kozhumbu* (spicy gravy), *keerai masiyal* (pureed spinach) and *sutta appalam* (roasted *paapad*) for dinner,' said Appa one day, during that trip. Where on earth? 'This is UP, Pa,' I said to him. 'It's better to have the local fare of *aalu* (potatoes), *dal* (lentils) and *roti*.' He gave the driver directions to go to an obscure place tucked between a dilapidated temple and a grocer's shop. A smoky board at the entrance said, in fading letters, 'Veg. meals ready: South Indian.' Don't ask how he knew this place existed, but the food was divine, made to order – we had to return in forty minutes after placing the order – home-cooked and fresh. That's where we went every day for our lunch and dinner. Dipping ourselves in the Ganga, visiting temples, roaming the streets of Hardwar and Rishikesh, we had a relaxed holiday from everything fast and frenetic, demanding and boring. I don't think Appa was particularly religious, but he did know a lot about faiths and was wont to respect different persuasions and places of worship.

Mediterranean cruise

Revathi, Kamala, Bobjima and I on board the cruise liner. Revathi and Kamala took Appa and Bobjima (and me) on a cruise of the Mediterranean to celebrate our parents' sixtieth wedding anniversary on 30 June 2000.

Growing up in Pudukkottai and the Ramakrishna Home in Chennai, he'd had a solid grounding in yoga and the scriptures. I remember every year he would go through the thread-changing ceremony, reciting the mantras even before the priest would utter them.

On one of our summer trips to Kodaikanal, the hill station close to Madurai, Appa took me one morning to visit the 'Palace', the summer home of the members of the Pudukkottai royal family. The three brothers – Periya Dorai, Nadu Dorai and Chinna Dorai – were relatives of Maharaja Rajagopala Thondaiman and the eldest of the three became next in line of ascendancy, as the Maharaja married an Australian and had a son, Sydney. At the Palace we were told Periya Dorai was in the workshop. We found the soft-spoken Periya Dorai admiring a Nataraja bronze he'd just finished making. We hardly saw Nadu Dorai, but Chinna Dorai and I have chatted many times during the annual regattas, boat races, at Kodai Lake, between cheering and booing participants.

As children, we eagerly looked forward to our annual summer holidays in Kodaikanal, for it meant hikes, picnics and games, walks around the lake, and boating. Appa would be in and out, as much as his shooting schedules permitted, and he took special interest in the garden and orchard. He was friends with Mrs Gombertz, the English lady who was our caretaker till she decided to move back to England. He would often chat with her as she wielded a garden tool, snipping away at withered flowers and leaves, peering through her glasses. Each summer she would invite us to her little cottage for English tea and scones, and she would entertain us with new toys and tricks her family had sent her from England.

Appa had bought the beautiful bungalow, called 'Redlynch', when I was studying in the third standard. Its previous owner was E. Hayward, of Hayward's Whisky fame, who shifted to Kodai after retirement, but was taken away by his family to the UK when he became too old to live alone. With gardens spread over three acres; it was a popular sightseeing stop for holidaymakers. During their years together, Savithri Aunty's family would be in Kodai, too, at 'Bina Pani', a house they'd bought close to the lake on the other side from where we lived.

Appa was a member of the English Club where he would play tennis and meet his friends. He was also a member of the Kodai Golf Club, from where he would bring home large omelets stuffed with tomatoes and onions. He would ask Bobjima to make tamarind paste (*pulikaachal*) with which tamarind rice is made, and invite people over to eat. We as children participated each year in the annual regatta at the Boat Club, of which too Appa was member, and Revathi and Kamala won several prizes in the singles and doubles races.

Take a break

Appa and Bobjima taking a break in Kodaikanal, their favourite summer destination. The entire family moved there during vacation time in school and college, for two whole months every year.

When Gigi was nine years old, Appa took her along to the pilgrimage to Sabarimalai in Kerala. This was his fourth trip to the shrine, undertaken after a forty-day ritual of fasting and austerities. Gigi remembers the experience fondly, 'After reaching the foothills, we had to walk the thirty-kilometer stretch to the temple and since I was yet a child, I would tire easily. Appa would lift me and put me on his shoulders and walk on, as we chanted '*kallum mullum kaaluku methai*' (stones and thorns are but soft mattresses for our feet), '*swamiye charanam Aiyappa*' (Lord Ayyappa, we surrender to you.)'

The last time Bobjima, Appa, Revathi, Kamala and I, along with Revathi and Kamala's spouses, went on a holiday, was in the year 2000. It was a special year, the sixtieth year of our parents' marriage, and the older girls had booked a Mediterranean cruise that began from Barcelona and ended in Istanbul. What a memorable trip that was. Gigi and her husband could not join us. We missed them, but enjoyed all the stopovers and sights at Barcelona, Monte Carlo, Athens, Naples, Venice, Kusadasi and Istanbul. Appa was almost eighty and not very energetic, but Bobjima was full of beans and even took him on her own by taxi to see the Leaning Tower of Pisa when we had left them behind on the ship, saying they would not be able to come on the tour. She bought a disposable camera and got them photographed, too. That was a real surprise.

CHAPTER SEVEN
The End

You are a child of the universe,
no less than the trees and the stars.

– Desiderata

As Appa approached his eightieth year, Kamala took over. He moved into the house she lived in and was well taken care of. Bobjima, now suffering frequent asthmatic problems, was taken care of, too, in G.G. Hospital. When Kamala shifted to her newly renovated home, Appa and Bobjima lived together in the house close to the hospital with twenty-four-hour nursing attendants and visiting relatives and friends. The four years before he passed away, Bobjima and Appa spent all their waking and sleeping hours together. They had a close relationship, symbiotic, more like siblings. They couldn't bear to be separated; they constantly worried about the other's well being, and spent most of their waking hours chatting or just being quiet together. Bobjima's frustration gave way to compassion and empathy; Appa became calmer and quieter. He would sit outside in the evenings, greeting people who filed into the hospital or chatting with his fans who were growing old, too. Appa was slowly growing weaker and quieter. One could say that was natural with advancing years. However, what really upset me was when he lost all interest in food. He, who reveled in cooking, serving, and tasting the day's cooking at the kitchens of friends and relatives, now showed absolutely no inclination to do so. He would sit in front of his plate, pushing bits of food around. In a few minutes he would be back, and the kitchen help would complain that no sooner had she cleared the table, he would be back, with another plate, and the ritual would get repeated. On one of my visits to Chennai I was upset to see Appa return to the plate – covered, left undisturbed where he'd left it – and peck at the cold, stale food. He'd simply lost his appetite. Viji would often make soup and bring it for him. Initially he would have it, but in later days he would just spit it out.

FACING PAGE:

His best friends

Appa seated by the puja mandap *with Misty and Sunny on his lap while an amused Bobjima looks on, at their home in Chennai. Both of them were dog-lovers.*

Renewal of vows

Following his eightieth birthday on 17 November 2000, Appa and Bobjima re-enact the wedding ceremony, on 30 November. In the picture, Revathi is helping Appa with the mangalsutra *ritual, as the couple is showered with flowers.*

His listlessness and the frequent pensive look were symptoms of physical discomfort, no doubt. His blood platelet count was falling, his haemoglobin was low for which he was being treated. What began as an occasional blood/platelet transfusion, once in two months or less, became a more frequent exercise until a time came when he was being given blood every week. Once his blood count plunged and he needed urgent rejuvenation. There was a shortage and Kamala immediately had a message asking for suitable donors flashed on a Tamil television news channel. The response was overwhelming. Relatives of fans, strangers, friends and well-wishers came forward to help, so much so that the supply exceeded the demand. He was now being given daily transfusions.

But the blood donations and good wishes could at best postpone the inevitable. Appa would protest, pleading, 'Why have you turned me into a pin cushion? Leave me alone. Let me go.'

Myelodysplastic syndrome is an old-age related blood disorder – the patient's red and white blood corpuscles and platelets get affected. The clotting mechanism falters and the patient suffers internal bleeding. Twice, Appa was admitted to the Intensive Care Unit of Apollo Hospital, Chennai, and brought back home when he improved. The third time, however, his organs began to fail. 'Appa, do you wish to go home?' asked Revathi, who 'knew' that the end was near. 'Yes, please take me home,' Appa whispered as he gesticulated.

The last few days were tragic and touching. A distressed Bobjima would keep asking the nurse, 'How is he? Any hope? Will he get better?' And the nurse would say, 'Amma, pray for him.' Appa would just lie in bed, with the drip on one arm and the other arm lying inert by his side, eyes closed. We took turns holding his hand and talking to him, but would get no response. Meanwhile, he was sinking, slowly.

Revathi was booked to return to the U.S. on 21 March 2005. She had already extended her leave, and now it was time to get back to her patients. It was a heart-rending scene. Packed and ready, baggage in the car, Revathi went to Appa's bedside, knowing fully well that this would be the last time she would see her dear father alive, and tried to say goodbye. She wept so much, and asked for his forgiveness for leaving him. There was no one available to fill in for her at her hospital. Appa, who had been lying inert all these days, suddenly lifted both his arms in a gesture that seemed to say, 'Don't worry, just go.' His eyes were still closed, he was breathing lightly, and slowly he put his arms down back on the bed. He was apparently conscious of all that was happening around him.

By the time Revathi's flight reached Chicago, her son Rajesh called her on her cell phone. 'Mummy, Appakutty has gone to God.' 'Okay,' she said. When she reached her home in Peoria, a two-hour drive from Chicago, she turned on a Tamil television channel and found herself watching a direct telecast of Appa's funeral at the electric crematorium.

When Appa breathed his last in the early hours of 22 March 2005, we were shattered. Though we consoled each other saying Appa had found peace at last, the tears wouldn't stop flowing. Appa would often say, 'My prayer to God is to please let me die in harness.' Well, his wish was granted, almost – he'd done a year-long television serial that ended in 2001. After that he and Bobjima had made trips to the U.S. where they had spent time with Revathi and her family for a few months at a time.

Bobjima missed Appa so much that she, too, lost the will to live. Eight months later, on 27 November the same year, she succumbed to an asthma attack. When the end came, she had been unconscious for a few days, and so she perhaps was unaware of her last moments.

A stream of visitors, VIPs and celebrities, actors and filmmakers, students and vegetable vendors, fans and friends, streamed in to pay their last respects to Appa as he lay in state in a glass case, covered by flowers. Some visitors went inside the house to meet Bobjima who was seated on her reclining sofa – she often napped in a semi-supine position because

Who says Gemini is dead?

Narayani Ganesh, a Senior Assistant Editor with The Times of India, remembers her father...

When Appa was lying in state just before he was to take the final trip into the electric crematorium, he was given a 30-gun salute by the Tamil Nadu police. My only thought at that moment was: Boy, would he love this! That was Appa through and through: He simply loved fuss and celebration. Even during the last few days when he was bedridden and critical, he would clasp my hand tightly and say weakly: "Scratch my head!" He had to be the centre of attraction.

I've often wondered, what endeared him so much to people across the board, including my mom. Appa was an incurable romantic. And he was handsome and charming. Even the chubby Irish nun who was the headmistress of the school I went to in Chennai was besotted by him. She would ruffle my hair when I was in junior school and ask: "Where is that little rascal, your father? What is he up to *now*? Ask him to come and see me!" He would flash a charming smile at her and spring to attention the moment she entered the room, bowing and greeting her with utmost courtesy. And she would be floored but still, would put on a strict expression and wag her finger, tut-tut ting at his "misdemeanors".

Appa loved spending summer vacations with the family in Kodaikanal, the hill station on Palani Hills. He fell in love with a house that belonged to a British gentleman, Mr Hayward. When the house was up for sale in the early '60s, Appa was the first to write to Mr Hayward, showing his interest. He wrote:

Dear Mr Hayward,
I was in Kodai recently, shooting a film and I happened to visit your bungalow, 'Redlynch'. I am so impressed. Redlynch has already found a place in my heart. I hear you plan to sell it. I would love to buy it from you. If you are indeed going to sell it, kindly consider my request favourably.

Yours faithfully,
Gemini Ganesan
PostScript: How do you have the heart to sell such a beautiful bungalow? If I were you, I would never let it slip from my fingers.

PTI

Filmstar Kamal Hasan pays tributes to Tamil actor Gemini Ganesan in Chennai on Tuesday. Ganesan's daughter Kamala Selvaraj is also seen.

The agent got in touch with Appa, drove a hard bargain and the house was sold to him. Later, the shrewd agent smiled and showed him the telegram Mr Hayward had sent: "Whatever the price quoted, the house should go only to Gemini Ganesan."

An elderly man shed tears at Appa's funeral. I asked him who he was and he said that 30 years ago, Appa found him pumping air in cycles on the road and helped him set up a cycle repair shop of his own. "He's my dear friend," he said, indignantly. I was touched. Who says Gemini is dead? He lives on in the hearts of his wife, children and other family members who doted on him, and also in the hearts of all those who came in contact with him over the years, professionally or otherwise. Gemini Ganesan's contribution to Indian cinema is a very small part of what he gave with great enthusiasm to thousands of people in little affectionate gestures, in compassion, in love, and in friendship. His reach went far, far beyond the silver screen. He was incorrigible, but was also so child-like and lovable. I tell my mother, I'm sure he is already working his charms on people up there in Heaven!

Gemini's death marks end of his love affair with life

By Nikhat Kazmi

Vaazhkai Padagu (The Boat of Life) may have sunk, but the ripples and the ro- ce of his life still remain. For, for nothing was Gemini 'Ra- wami' Ganesan anointed *al Mannan*, the King of Ro- ce.

ere was a man who played the y of love, not only in his films in real life too. The tangled , the dreamy eyes and the n-struck demeanour made the perfect *Pyaar ka Devta* in 200-plus films he did in Tamil, gu, Malayalam and Hindi. in real life too, where he married four women, the first at the of 19. His death, at 84, on sday morning, due to renal ure, has not only ended his t love affair with life, but also ks the end of a chapter in th Indian cinema. For, Gemi- Ganesan was the last of the lywood Mohicans which in- led legendary actors like MG chandran and Sivaji Gane- in the Triumvirate.

as it a coincidence that even last noteworthy film, *Avvai nmukhi*, saw him playing a -struck widower who falls in with his grand daughter's

governess (Kamal Haasan in drag)? Yes, we are talking about the Tamil original of the Hindi re-make *Chachi 420* where he essayed the role that was replicated by Amrish Puri. His greatest hits — *Penn, Kanavane Kankanda Deivam, Missiamma, Vanjikottal Valiban* — have all seen him playing and perfecting the art of romance with his screen partners like Vyjayanthimala, Sowcar Janaki, Devika and Savitri. And often, his celluloid affair would carry over into real life too...He married two of his screen partners, Savitri and Pushpavalli, the mother of Rekha.

Interestingly, Gemini Ganesan's film career stretches across a time span that can be measured in terms of independent Indian history. A chemistry lecturer in Madras Christian College, Ramaswami Ganesan joined Gemini Studios as a production executive on August 15, 1947. He not only earned his livelihood from the studio but got his nom de plume — Gemini — too. His first big break came at the age of 30 and he was catapulted to star status with films like *Penn* and *Kanavane Kankanda Deivam*. Unlike MGR and Sivaji Ganesan, his co-actors, Gemini never showed an inclination for politics and led a private life. He was awarded the Padma Shri in 1971 and penned an autobiography, *Vaazkhai Padagu* (The Boat of Life).

Today, film buffs will remember him for his nine roles as an 'innocent' beguiling philanderer in *Naan Avanillai*. The actor was 54 when he played the title role of the debonair deceiver who changes his identity to lure pretty women. And they all succumbed to his charms, as did his young secretary whom he married at the age of 81.

FACING PAGE:

Remembrance and report

We'd come back home after saying goodbye to Appa at the electric crematorium at Besant Nagar in Chennai. As I stepped out of the bath, a colleague from the Times of India, *Delhi, phoned to ask if I could write something on my father for the coming issue. 'The editor was asking, but only if you feel up to it,' he added. When I told Kamala, she marched me off to the computer and shut the door as it was a narrow deadline. This is a cutting of that report in the TOI issue dated 23 March 2005.*

LEFT:

Moving obituary

TOI's film critic, Nikhat Kazmi, wrote an obituary that was published on 23 March 2005. The print media published extensive reports and articles, and southern television channels telecast his films for several weeks at a stretch.

she had trouble breathing – looking quite dazed and yet, smilingly receiving all who came to her. When Kamal Haasan walked in, Kamala said to her, 'See, who has come, Appa's other son.'

Actress Sowcar Janaki spoke warmly of Appa and said he was like a brother to her, that he was a fine human being and full of compassion. Jayalalithaa, who was then the Chief Minister of Tamil Nadu, was gracious and remembered her meeting with him only a few weeks ago when they exchanged pleasantries.

Two weeks after Appa left us, his first grandson Rajesh, Revathi's son, wrote the following email to his cousins and aunts:

Remembering Appakutty

I don't think that I ever knew Gemini Ganesan the actor, the film icon, the superstar. Rather, I only knew the jovial, loquacious, animated man, my grandfather, Appakutty.

I left Madras for the U.S.A. with my family at the age of three, to return as a seven-year-old on a short visit. I remember feeling quite scared at the airport, the hustle and bustle, the disarray...

Appakutty and Rajesh

Appa with first grandchild Rajesh (Revathi and Swaminathan's son) in the U.S. Reproduced here is the nostalgic letter Rajesh wrote to us via email after Appa's passing away. On the facing page is a poem – looks like a rough draft – Appa wrote on the occasion of Rajesh's medical graduation in 1997, but never sent to him.

My Mom and I were scurrying about to get our luggage. My mom told me, 'I'll be right back.' I sat holding the handles of my bag, waiting for my mom to return. I felt as if I were in an alien world, despite being back in the place of my birth... And there he was.

He was shouting and waving, in the distance. My mother seemed to have forgotten about me... She was calling out, 'AAAPPPAAAA...AAAAAPPPPAA.'

Why was Mom shouting? What was the fuss about? I couldn't figure it out... until this handsome, burly man scooped me into his arms and kissed me on the cheek.

A brush with a thin, well-attended-to moustache would be my eager call to welcome every time I visited Madras thereafter. A welcome that would tickle my face, every time.

We would visit India every couple of years. Upon our arrival there, or upon Appakutty's arrival to the States, I would look forward to and yearn for that 'prickly' welcome.

It was not until I was much older that I came to know of his stature in south Indian cinema, his eclectic style of acting, and his deep love and affection for his entire family. The relationships that he had with his loved ones transcended any barriers that we all would seemingly perceive.....

I wish that I could have spoken to him more often. Appakutty had the ability to speak to anyone about anything, and would be the first to chastise himself, before anyone else. 'Keep yourself busy,' he would say. 'Work sincerely, or not at all.' These words I keep with me, to this day.

Appakutty lived a full life, or so they say, and he was blessed enough to be able to meet his great-grandchildren. Yet, towards the end, he was not at peace; he yearned for the glory of yesteryears. This too, has taught us, that at life's end, one must be content with everything – with family, with vocation, and ultimately and unequivocally, with God.

It is my belief that he has found this peace. I will miss him dearly. I will make it a point to tell my children of the wonderful journey that was his life. His legend lives on in them, and in those to come.

– Rajesh Swaminathan, 10 April 2005

Gemini Ganesh

6. Nungambakkam High Road,
Madras 600 034 S. India
Phone : 479630

Congratulations Raj!

Life is to live with steps of graduation,
Measured steps, not mincing steps without deviation
One should go gradually up the ladder
To reach great heights of calibred cadre

A graduated living shows us to think,
Of calculated moves with no time to blink;
Milestones ~~one~~ crosses to reach destination,
Ambitious ones have in mind that intention.

Success one often gets by jumping hurdles,
Of course he crosses the intervening puddles;
And now Nagaraj R. Iyer has won the laurel,
For boarding in his fame medical knowledge good;

Right now he should start showing,
The medical tricks he is zealously guarding;
To serve humanity at large in distress,
Suffering from pain, disease and stress.

Raj the great should really wear the crown
As living Hippocrates the legend renown.
To bring kudos to ~~an~~ a blend exemplary home
with Ram, Laxmi, Brign, Rajathy and him wonders one done

Epilogue

Through humour, you can soften some of the worst blows that life delivers. And once you find laughter, no matter how painful your situation might be, you can survive it.

– Bill Cosby

On my now infrequent visits to Chennai, it is often Nallasamy, Appa's driver of many years, who comes to the airport to take me home. He now works for Kamala and his duties are mostly to do with her grandchildren. Does he miss 'Aiyaa' (Sir)? It took me five long years after Appa's demise to pop this question. In reply, he inserted a CD into the stereo, filling the car with music from Appa's popular films. Tears coursed down his cheeks as he nodded his head. I fell silent. What was it about Appa that evoked such deep feelings in near and dear ones?

Appa was affectionate. He had a compassionate and trusting nature. Yet he was by no means perfect, and he did not project himself as being so. He was frugal in spending on himself, but didn't think twice before buying homes for his employees and encouraging their children through school or college. He would lose his temper but would always make up for it with kind gestures. His conversations with them were those of equals, never patronizing. Perhaps that was what really mattered.

As a family, we four sisters are pretty close though we are separated by geography. Our relationships with our other siblings we didn't grow up with – Rekha and Radha, Viji and Sathish – have always been cordial, though not exactly close. Viji and I were friends because we spent a lot of time together as children, though as grown-ups we did not interact much as we had our own lives and responsibilities. If we're all now in frequent touch, visiting, telephoning and emailing each other, it is largely because of Kamala. She makes a conscious effort to maintain close family ties even though we were raised in different homes. Even Appa could not have imagined that all his children would one day have mature and comfortable relationships with each other, while respecting the other's space.

FACING PAGE:

Shaking a leg

Octogenarian Appakutty dancing with some of his children and grandchildren at a party organized before Kamala's daughter Priya's wedding at bridegroom Sanjay's home in November 2001. Left to right: The bride Priya, Prasanna, Appakutty, Kamala, Viji, her daughter-in-law Madhuvanti, and Sonali.

Stamp and First Day Cover

The Indian Posts and Telegraph Department released a commemorative postage stamp as tribute to Gemini Ganesan on 2 February 2006. At the function, Appa's colleagues from the film industry, his friends and family shared their memories and paid their tributes.

During Appa and Bobjima's last days, whether it was Radha and Sathish from the U.S., Rekha from Mumbai or Viji in Chennai, every one of them would make it a point to visit and seek the blessings of not just Appa but Bobjima as well. Though our parents are no longer alive, the tradition of meeting and greeting continues.

For Revathi and Kamala, life after Appa has meant recounting his memories every single day – either by watching his films, listening to his songs, talking about him, or simply calling each other up and shedding a few tears – despite their busy schedules as medical professionals. Perhaps their closeness comes from having spent more quality time with Appa during their childhood and adolescence, and the fact that they were taking care of both Appa and Bobjima by turn, during their last days. Kamala takes an active interest in participating in tributes to Appa, whether on television or at functions; she makes the effort to stay in touch with Appa's friends, colleagues and associates and invites them to all special family occasions. Gigi feels Appa's and Bobjima's absence deeply since memorabilia surrounds her in the home she grew up in.

I tend to recollect all the funny moments I've had with Appa and Bobjima – when we laughed together or goofed up on something that made us look silly. I cannot bring myself to watch his films for more than a few seconds, as I find it saddens me and that's not how I wish to feel about either of my parents. Both were witty in their own way and to a large extent it was their sense of humour that kept their spirits, and ours, up most of the time.

RIGHT:

Lost and found

'All that is not given is lost,' wrote Appa on 15 January 1996 to S. Chandrasekhar, manager of the bookstore, Higginbothams, in Chennai – gifting him an expensive shaver. (Chandrasekhar had ribbed him, saying, 'Aren't you supposed to be a kanjoos *(miser)?')*

BOTTOM:

Last time in Delhi

A frail Bobjima and Appa during their last visit to Delhi in January 2002.

The Bobjima-Ganesan Family, 2003

Standing left to right: Rajesh carrying his third child, Sohil, my younger daughter Sonali, Priya and Sanjay, Gigi's daughter Ganga, Geeta and Shreedhar Rajan.

Seated left to right: My older daughter Maya, me, Kamala, Appa, Bobjima, Revathi, Jaya (Gigi), Swaminathan.

Rajesh and Geeta's second child, Sohaan, is on Appa's lap. Priya and Sanjay's first daughter, Neharikka, is on Bobjima's lap. Standing behind my parents is Selina, their first great-grandchild and Rajesh's first child.

The photo was taken by the pool in Kamala's beach-house in Chennai. My parents were both unwell those days but since their grandchildren from the U.S. were visiting India for the first time, the moment was captured.

Narayani, My Girlchild Sweet!

Narayani, my girlchild sweet,
Does things pretty, to give us a treat;
Whatever she does, beaming and smiling,
Makes all things steaming and shining
Qualities she possesses as an exemplar,
Making her so lovable and popular...

Doctrine of Karma of Gita from Chinmaya
Should have given her strength and Maya,
Amidst the chaos and confusion she sings coolly,
To amuse her children, Maya and Sonali,
With flights and phones Ab Dilli Door Nahin Hain,
Often we phone, fly or detrain to say "Hi!"

My child has braved many a torrent,
Has learned to swim against the current;
The current can hope no more to shock
Because she has friends who do stop,
Narayani has much confidence in her
May God Bless her always, Hear, Hear!

2 October 1988

Gemini Ganesan